Groundwork for the
Metaphysics of Morals

Grundlegung

zur

Metaphysik

der Sitten

von

Immanuel Kant.

Riga,

bey Johann Friedrich Hartknoch

1785.

Groundwork for the Metaphysics of Morals

IMMANUEL KANT

Edited and translated by Allen W. Wood

With an updated translation, introduction, and notes

Yale
UNIVERSITY PRESS

New Haven & London

First published by Yale University Press in 2002 as a volume in the Rethinking the Western Tradition series. This edition, with an updated translation, introduction, and notes, published by Yale University Press in 2018.

Yale University Press books may be purchased in quantity for educational, business, or promotional use. For information, please e-mail sales.press@yale.edu (U.S. office) or sales@yaleup.co.uk (U.K. office).

Set in Times Roman type by Newgen North America, Austin, Texas.
Printed in the United States of America.
10 9 8 7 6 5 4 3 2 1
Library of Congress Control Number: 2017952054
ISBN 978-0-300-22743-7 (paper : alk. paper)

A catalogue record for this book is available from the British Library.
This paper meets the requirements of
ANSI/NISO z39.48-1992 (Permanence of Paper).

To Rega

once again and always

Contents

Abbreviations

Citations of Kant's Writings

Ak	*Immanuel Kants Schriften.* Ausgabe der königlich preussischen Akademie der Wissenschaften (Berlin: W. de Gruyter, 1902), cited by volume:page number in this edition
Ca	*Cambridge Edition of the Writings of Immanuel Kant* (New York: Cambridge University Press, 1992–2016); this edition provides marginal Ak volume:page citations
Anth	*Anthropologie in pragmatischer Hinsicht* (1798), Ak 7 *Anthropology from a Pragmatic Point of View,* Ca *Anthropology, History, and Education*
BM	*Von der Buchmacherei* (1797), Ak 8 *On Turning Out Books,* Ca *Anthropology, History, and Education*
G	*Grundlegung zur Metaphysik der Sitten* (1785), Ak 4 *Grundlegung zur Metaphysik der Sitten* (1785–86), edited by Bernd Kraft and Dieter Schönecker (Hamburg: Felix Meiner Verlag, 1999)
I	*Idee zu einer allgemeinen Geschichte in weltbürgerlicher Absicht* (1784), Ak 8 *Idea Toward a Universal History with a Cosmopolitan Aim,* Ca *Anthropology, History, and Education*
KpV	*Kritik der praktischen Vernunft* (1788), Ak 5 *Critique of Practical Reason,* Ca *Practical Philosophy*
KrV	*Kritik der reinen Vernunft* (1781, 1787), cited by A/B pagination *Critique of Pure Reason,* Ca *Critique of Pure Reason*
KU	*Kritik der Urteilskraft* (1790), Ak 5 *Critique of the Power of Judgment,* Ca *Critique of the Power of Judgment*
MA	*Mutmaßlicher Anfang der Menschengeschichte* (1786), Ak 8

Formulas of the Moral Law

Kant formulates the moral law in three principal ways. The first and third
of these have variants which are intended to bring the law "closer to intuition" and make it easier to apply. These five principal formulations of the
moral law will be abbreviated as follows.

First formula:

FUL   *The Formula of Universal Law: "Act only in accordance with
that maxim through which you at the same time can will that
it become a universal law"* (G 4:421; cf. G 4:402), with its
variant,

FLN   *The Formula of the Law of Nature: "So act, as if the maxim of
your action were to become through your will a **universal law
of nature**"* (G 4:421; cf. G 4:436).

Second formula:

FH   *The Formula of Humanity as End in Itself: "So act that you
use humanity, as much in your own person as in the person
of every other, always at the same time as an end and never
merely as a means"* (G 4:429; cf. G 4:436).

Third formula:

FA   *Formula of Autonomy: "*. . . the idea *of the will of every
rational being as a will giving universal law"* (G 4:431; cf.
G 4:432) or "Not to choose otherwise than so that the maxims
of one's choice are at the same time comprehended with it in
the same volition as universal law" (G 4:440; cf. G 4:432, 434,
438), with its variant,

FRE   *The Formula of the Realm of Ends:* "Act in accordance with
maxims of a universally legislative member for a merely
possible realm of ends" (G 4:439; cf. G 4:433, 437, 438).

Translator's Introduction

Kant's little book of 1785 is among the most significant texts in the history of ethics. For over two centuries it has been a standard of reference—sometimes a model to be developed and expanded on, sometimes a target of criticism, often something of both. It has served these purposes for the German idealist and German Romantic traditions, for Victorians of the utilitarian school such as Mill and Sidgwick, for later British idealists such as Green and Bradley, for the neo-Kantians, for twentieth-century philosophers in both the continental and the Anglophone traditions, and for moral philosophers of all persuasions right down to the present day.

The depth and originality of the ideas contained in the *Groundwork* no doubt merit this influence. It is a famous book, but also a difficult and even obscure book, which is hard to understand and easy to misunderstand. (I am not kidding when I tell classes I teach that I did not understand it at all the first fifty times I read it.) Much of the *Groundwork*'s influence has been based on common misunderstandings of what it actually says. Moreover, in the development of Kant's own moral thinking, the *Groundwork* occupies a place that ought to make us question the wisdom of treating it, as moral philosophers customarily do, as if taken all by itself it could be treated as a definitive statement of Kant's views on ethics.

In many ways, it is precisely the scholarly emphasis on this book, along with Kant's other foundational work in ethics, the *Critique of Practical Reason,* that has led to most of the misunderstandings of Kantian ethics that still prevail among moral philosophers. Readers have often brought to the *Groundwork* a set of expectations that do not match Kant's narrow aims in that work. It and the second *Critique* are *foundational* works, not works about particular ethical problems or about moral psychology. Kant has interesting views about many of those topics too, but he does not present them in the writings for which he has become best known.

When readers of the *Groundwork* have taken what they found there as if it were a set of answers to questions Kant is not asking in that book, Kant's responses to his own questions are easily misunderstood. This is especially true of Kant's claim, early in the work, that beneficence from duty has a distinctive moral worth not found in beneficence from mere sympathy or inclination. Based on a misunderstanding of both the meaning of this claim and its role in Kant's argument, readers form a common image of Kant as the representative of a kind of inhuman moralism, an attitude of moral rigidity and hostility to all the more tender human emotions. This image is conspicuously at odds with things Kant actually says in other writings, such as the *Metaphysics of Morals* (1797–1798), and even with some things he says in the *Groundwork* itself. But readers who began with the *Groundwork* tend to notice, and to emphasize, those parts of Kant's ethical theory that reinforce the false image of Kantian ethics they have gotten from misreading the *Groundwork* and to ignore everything that should lead them to question that image.

There is indeed something genuinely icy about the *Groundwork*. But it is misunderstood if it is perceived as the cold and unemotional temperament of its author. What it is instead is the cool intellect of a philosopher whose attention is focused on the most abstract questions of ultimate foundations. The chill winds that blow at us out of the *Groundwork* have their real source in philosophical perplexities about the grounds of reason, obligation, value, and freedom that lie at the deepest roots of our problematic human condition. If you don't like the *Groundwork,* then what you probably really don't like is pure unadulterated *philosophy*—and the unsettling, disorienting effect that fundamental philosophical questions are likely to have on you. Most likely you prefer a more popular and comforting set of moral reflections. If so, your tastes are perfectly healthy ones. But the deeper philosophical questions will still be there to disturb you, if you ever think about them. And you should not let a misreading of the *Groundwork* be the way you express your preferences.

It does not help that Kant was writing for an eighteenth-century audience, whose moral attitudes, and even their attitudes toward morality as a whole, were in many ways very different from ours. Their assumptions were often less critical of appeals to morality and less skeptical of the psychic health of such appeals than anyone could be in a culture downwind from Marx, Nietzsche, and Freud. The moral enthusiasm Kant derived from Rousseau only intensified these assumptions. The combination of Kant's taking for granted the moral attitudes of his time and the chilly abstractness of his focus on the ultimate philosophical foundations of morality can be a toxic combination. Many features of Kant's basic system of values might counteract the resulting stereotype, such as his emphasis on the equal dignity of all persons and the importance of free self-government and mutual respect in their interactions. So might his application of these values in other writings. This would include the often overlooked importance of feeling in Kant's moral psychology and the importance Kant attaches to friendship in the moral life. It also includes the flexibility of Kantian morality based on the importance it accords to *judgment:* the application of moral rules and concepts differently, to different situations, and the acceptance of possibly irresolvable controversy in such matters.

What Kant was hoping, of course, is that your reading of the *Groundwork* would change your mind about the foundations of ethics—this is what the book was supposed to do—and even lead you to rethink your own approach to issues the *Groundwork* itself does not address. But that's a lot to expect of a reader, and it is unsurprising that most readers have not been up to the challenge.

I realize it will not come as welcome news to those new to the study of Kant's ethics to be told that the *Groundwork* does not offer them the whole of Kant's moral philosophy, especially its answers to the kinds of questions most of us naturally bring to a work of moral philosophy. Readers might have hoped to obtain a full understanding of Kant's moral philosophy just by reading this one famous little book. But there is no getting around the fact that Kant is a difficult philosopher. He was a very poor (sometimes a downright disastrous) popularizer of his own thought. There is no easy path to its appropriation. Maybe you will need to read the *Groundwork* many times (as I had to) before you begin to understand it. What I'm trying to do now is shorten the process.

The *Groundwork* is still indeed the right starting place for understanding Kantian ethics, but if you want to understand Kant's ethics, you cannot stop with it. You should not expect to find an entire moral philosophy in this famous little book, especially not Kant's. If all you read of Kant's ethics is the *Groundwork,* then you must carefully limit the conclusions you draw in ways that correspond to the text's limited aims. If you do discipline yourself in that way, you probably should conclude that what you've read gives you only an abstract and impoverished look at Kantian ethics. You might then not think it was worth the trouble to read so difficult a text only to get so little out of it. I am not trying to argue you out of this sense of disappointment, but again, only to help you understand the *Groundwork* correctly, if you set that as your aim.

The good news for Kant scholarship is that the increasing emphasis in the last generation on Kant's other ethical writings, especially his late work the *Metaphysics of Morals,* has begun to correct the traditional misunderstandings of Kantian ethics. Also helpful is the fact that in recent years, there have been a number of good commentaries on the *Groundwork:* those by Jens Timmermann and Henry Allison, as well as the commentary (now available in the English as well as the German version) that I have co-authored with Dieter Schönecker, and also my Cambridge Element on Kant's Formulas of the Moral Law. These recent writings are listed, along with a select bibliography of other readings, at the end of this volume.

The *Groundwork* in Kant's philosophical development

It may help readers new to the *Groundwork* to understand its place in Kant's life-history as a philosopher. The last decade of Kant's writings (1788–1798, when he was in his mid-sixties to mid-seventies) was dominated by works about ethics, politics, and religion. But Kant's interest in philosophy did not begin with these subjects at all. He began as what we would now call a "natural scientist"—what would then have been a called a *natural philosopher.* His focus was entirely on physics, astronomy, chemistry, and what we would now call geology or "earth sciences" (in whose invention Kant can even claim some share). Kant became a *philosopher* in our sense of the word only when he began to worry about the epistemological foundations of these sciences, and also how they relate to questions of metaphysics—especially to the theoretical proofs for the existence of God and the proper (and improper) use of the idea of divine design or purposiveness in understanding nature.

In 1764 Kant was still a virtually unknown *Privatdozent* at the University of Königsberg—that is, he was licensed to teach, but paid no salary by the university. He had to make a meager living from the fees he could charge students for attending his lectures. That year Kant submitted a prize essay to the Prussian Academy of Sciences whose title was *Inquiry Concerning the Distinctness of the Principles of Natural Theology and Morality.* This essay won second prize, first prize going to Moses Mendelssohn (1729–1786) for his elegantly written essay expounding the then dominant metaphysical position of Christian Wolff (1679–1754). The relatively brief discussion of moral philosophy in Kant's prize essay reveals a strong attraction to the moral sense theory of the Scottish philosopher Francis Hutcheson (1694–1747). That may be surprising, because Kant was soon to reject Hutcheson's approach and to identify his own moral philosophy as a "metaphysics of morals"—a term implying that the foundation of ethics lies in reason rather than in sense or feeling. We clearly see Kant distancing himself from Hutcheson in the First Section of the *Groundwork,* where he cites the rational motive of duty rather than natural sympathy as what gives true or genuine moral worth to actions. For this very reason, however, we should take special care to notice the subtle ways in which Kant always remained a Hutchesonian, retaining an important place in his ethics for moral feeling. In the *Groundwork,* this takes the form of his emphasis on the feeling of *respect* (G 4:401,n). Later it involves a variety of *rational* feelings: not only respect but also love for human beings (*philanthropia*), and approval or disapproval of our actions, and of ourselves (feelings of conscience). These feelings result, according to Kant, from the direct influence of moral reason on our sensibility (KpV 5:71–89; MS 6:399–403).

Kant's new-found interest in ethics in the mid-1760s was also inspired by his reading of Jean-Jacques Rousseau's famous writings of 1762: *On the Social Contract* and *Émile, or On Education.* It is difficult to overestimate the importance of Rousseau's influence on Kant's moral philosophy. It is from Rousseau that Kant gets many central features of his moral outlook. These include his deeply skeptical attitude toward people's moral self-assessments (G 4:407), his conviction that the cultivation of reason leads humanity sooner to misery than happiness (G 4:395–396), his implicit trust in the moral common sense of the ordinary (even the uneducated) human being (G 4:403–405), his conviction of the equal dignity of all rational beings (G 4:427–430), his grounding of morality on freedom of the will (G 4:446–450), and his conception of moral freedom or autonomy as that which releases us from the slavery of appetite through obedience to a law we give ourselves (G 4:431, 440; cf. Rousseau, *On the Social Contract,* I/8). Legend has it that in Kant's austerely furnished study, the only decoration was a portrait of Rousseau which hung over his writing desk.

How Kant finally came to write the *Groundwork*

Kant first gave notice of his intention to produce a system of moral philosophy under the title "metaphysics of morals" about 1768. It took him another eighteen years to deliver even a first, tentative installment of that ethical system, in the form of the little book here translated. Kant's title indicates its tentativeness: He was only *laying the ground for a metaphysics of morals* by seeking out and establishing morality's supreme principle. Readers of the *Groundwork* should always keep in mind this narrow aim. Kant is not yet trying to answer all the questions of ethics. If we try to use the *Groundwork* to get Kantian answers to all the questions we may bring to moral philosophy—especially if these are *our* questions to begin with, and not questions ever central to Kant's interests—we will be led astray, as readers of the *Groundwork* have often been for well over two centuries.

Apparently Kant began working on his little book late in 1783. Letters written at this time by Kant's brilliant but eccentric friend J. G. Hamann (1730–1788) report that he began writing about moral philosophy in order to provide an "anticritique" of a 1783 book on Cicero's treatise *De Officiis* by the German Enlightenment philosopher Christian Garve (1742–1798). According to Hamann, during the spring of 1784 Kant's critical discussion of Garve on Cicero was transformed into something different: what Hamann called a "Prodromus der Moral" (Ak 4:626–628). The title *Grundlegung zur Metaphysik der Sitten* is first mentioned in a letter from Hamann in September 1784.

Hamann's correspondence reveals him to be an avid Kant-watcher, sometimes a helpfully critical one. But there is also reason to be skeptical about his account of the genesis of the *Groundwork*. Hamann's account has inspired scholars as reputable as Klaus Reich and H. J. Paton to seek in the contents of the *Groundwork* for allusions to Cicero, and even to think that they have found them. But there are no explicit references there either to Cicero or to Garve's book about him. Garve was clearly a philosopher Kant respected. Kant was no doubt drawn to the subject of ethics at just this time by reading and reflecting on Garve's book or Cicero's classical treatise. Just as the *Groundwork* contains implicit criticisms of a Hutchesonian approach to moral philosophy, so it is also sharply critical of the eudaimonism that Kant found in Garve, which he criticized more explicitly eight years later (TP 8:278–289). But it seems to me unlikely that the *Groundwork,* as we now have it, could have grown merely out of a critical discussion of Garve on Cicero.

What Hamann calls the "Prodromus der Moral" would seem to be a project independent of any "anticritique" of Garve that Kant could have been undertaking. Kant was certainly working on other topics in 1784 whose affinity with the ethical theory presented in the *Groundwork* is also worth examining. For instance, he was reviewing Herder's *Ideas for the Philosophy of History of Humanity,* and writing two other short essays, *Idea for a Universal History from a Cosmopolitan Standpoint* and *Answer to the Question: What Is Enlightenment?* These essays reflect on human history, the social sources of the evil in human nature, the role of autonomous reason in directing our lives, and the rational prospects for the moral progress of the human species. The *Groundwork* was above all clearly the first down-payment, so to speak, on a very old promissory note—the first installment of the project in moral philosophy he had been entertaining for nearly twenty years.

The *Groundwork* went into press with Johann Hartknoch of Riga late in 1784. Throughout the winter and into the spring of 1785, Kant's followers waited impatiently for its appearance (Ak 4:628). The first copies were apparently available on April 7. A second edition, altered in a number of passages throughout (but never very greatly in any of them) appeared in 1786. Six more re-printings of this second edition of the work took place during Kant's lifetime.

The *Groundwork* and Kant's later ethical writings

Kant seems always to have treated the *Groundwork* as a successful laying of the ground for the ethical theory presented in his later writings. But clearly he soon came to regard it as not providing a complete or wholly clear presentation even of the foundations of his system. Only three years later he wrote a *Critique of Practical Reason* (1788) with the aim of clarifying those foundations, also correcting misunderstandings and answering criticisms of his moral philosophy that had come from early readers of the *Groundwork*. It is a matter of controversy how far what is said in the second *Critique* involves doctrinal revisions of the *Groundwork*. Many scholars think (though I myself doubt it) that Kant's references to our consciousness of the moral law as a "fact of reason" (KpV 5:31–32, 42–50) supplant the argument of the Third Section, offering an alternative to the *Groundwork*'s way of arguing for freedom of the will and relating freedom to the moral law.

As I have already mentioned, in the following decade Kant wrote a number of essays and treatises on topics involving the application of his moral philosophy to politics, history, international relations, education, and religion. But it was only after he had actually retired from university teaching, and perhaps as he began to realize that his mental powers were beginning to fail him, that he finally assembled from the notes and drafts of many years a work he called the "metaphysics of morals" and permitted it to be published as one of his very last works. And as I've already said, this supposedly more definitive treatment of a wider range of ethical issues has never been as influential in the reception of Kantian ethics as the foundational works of the 1780s.

Kant's essays and treatises of the 1790s, and especially the *Metaphysics of Morals,* give us explicit accounts of many matters on which readers of the *Groundwork* customarily try to deduce the "Kantian view" (by "triangulation," as it were) from what he says in this little foundational treatise. As I've already implied, many doctrines standardly attributed to Kant on this basis involve faulty trigonometry. Inferences commonly drawn from the *Groundwork* about "Kantian" views on such topics as the nature of moral motivation, the relation between reason and feeling in human action, the structure of everyday moral reasoning, and the nature of the will's freedom do not harmonize with what Kant actually says about these topics in the *Metaphysics of Morals, Religion Within the Boundaries of Mere Reason,* or other later works. In my judgment, this is seldom because Kant changed his mind after the *Groundwork,* and more frequently because readers have systematically misunderstood the *Groundwork*—sometimes then projecting these same misunderstandings onto their readings of the later writings as well.

The *Groundwork*'s aims and strategy

The aims of this short treatise are limited to the *search for* and *establishment of* the supreme principle of morality (G 4:392). Kant is not interested here in *applying* the principle. He provides *illustrations* of it only to make the principle intelligible to us, not to furnish a general criterion of right and wrong action, or provide a decision procedure for ethical choice. In fact, Kant does not even believe there are such things as these. The closest he comes to offering them is found in his theory of moral virtue in the *Metaphysics of Morals.* It includes a taxonomical sketch of moral duties as a way of expounding his account of virtue and vice. We see clearly in that work that Kant's ethics offers no general "universalizability test" for deciding which actions or maxims are right and which wrong. When readers of the *Groundwork* have thought that Kantian ethics is about some such thing, they have misread even those passages in the *Groundwork* itself that inspired their wild errors.

FIRST SECTION: THE MORAL PRINCIPLE FROM THE STANDPOINT OF THE ORDINARY MORAL AGENT

Kant, following Rousseau, holds that that the ordinary human being already has not only the intellectual capacity to distinguish right from wrong, but even can do this as well as any philosopher. Kant calls this "common rational moral cognition" (G 4:393). Consequently, he thinks that ordinary moral agents do not need a philosophical principle to give them knowledge of what they ought to do (G 4:403–405). Instead, Kant thinks that ordinary moral agents might need the help of philosophy in correcting the distortions of judgment in the application of moral concepts and duties to a particular situation. That's because all of us are apt to be misled by self-love and inclination into adapting the demands of morality to our needs, desires, and wishes (G 4:405). Kant's aim in the First Section is therefore to formulate a moral principle that offers an abstract or theoretical account of what moral agents do when they correct these corrupt tendencies in themselves by taking the universal standpoint of reason judging how to apply moral duties in particular cases. In Kant's view, they correct their judgment in this way without consciously employing any abstract reasoning procedure.

The sole function of the first formula of the moral law is to serve as such a "standard of judgment" (G 4:402–405). This formula does not supply the general duties it applies through judgment. These are assumed to be known by the ordinary moral agent through "common rational moral cognition."

Kant's strategy in developing the principle expressed in sound judgment is to focus on those specific cases in which a person will conform to duty only through having to be self-constrained through the thought of a moral law. This explains his focus on that special kind of moral worth he thinks ordinary agents will agree belongs only to actions done *from duty*—that is, *with moral self-constraint.* Thus he formulates the moral principle as demanding only that we must act in such a way that we could will the principle of our action to be a norm valid universally for everyone. This principle demands that we take the universal standpoint in judging how to apply an assumed duty to a particular case where we are tempted to exempt ourselves from the duty in a way that indulges our self-love or our inclinations.

This is as far as Kant means to get in the First Section of the *Groundwork,* because in his view it is only this far that ordinary moral agents need moral philosophy at all.

SECOND SECTION: THE PRINCIPLE OF MORALITY AND THE PHILOSOPHICAL CONCEPT OF THE WILL

In the Second Section, Kant leaves behind the standpoint of "common rational moral cognition" and moves to the level of moral philosophy itself. This is where his new foundation for moral *philosophy* really begins. Kant lays this foundation by first examining the different standards of reason in its practical use. He divides these standards into three: First, there is *instrumental* (or technical) reason, which requires us to choose those actions that serve as effective means to whatever ends we have chosen. Next, there is *prudential* (or pragmatic) reason, which counsels us to combine our empirical ends into a single whole (under the name of 'happiness') and to pursue it. Finally, there is *moral* reason, which commands us to do or refrain from certain actions simply for its own sake, irrespective of our happiness or any other ends we may have set at our discretion. A rational principle that presupposes an independently given end Kant calls a 'hypothetical imperative', because its rational constraint is conditional on that end. Instrumental and prudential reason issue hypothetical imperatives. A principle that commands us to do certain things without presupposing such ends is called a 'categorical imperative'. Moral reason issues categorical imperatives.

Kant's strategy in the Second Section is to derive the moral principle from the mere *concept* of a categorical imperative. He does this in three distinct ways, by distinguishing the *form* of the moral principle from its *matter* and then combining the two in a *complete* formulation. The form is the principle's universal bindingness; the matter is the end or substantive value which provides the motivating ground or reason why we should obey a categorical imperative. Kant represents the universal bindingness of the moral law as the requirement that actions should be chosen from the universal standpoint of reason. This requires that the maxim or subjective principle of the action is one the agent can will to be a universal law. This is the same formula as the one arrived at in the First Section (G 4:421, cf. G 4:402). But then Kant introduces a more "intuitive" variant of the first formula: this universal legislation is thought of as analogous to laws of nature. The agent's maxim ought to be such that it can be both thought and willed as a universal law of nature (G 4:421). Kant illustrates this variant formulation with four famous examples, which we will discuss a bit later.

The matter of the law, which grounds the second formula, is called an *end*. An end, in the most general sense of the term, is anything *for the sake of which* we act. It constitutes a standard or norm for our action, since actions must serve their ends. The matter of the moral law is not an end to be produced or effected; it is not anything we seek to bring about. Every action has an end to be effected because we always act for the sake of the intended results of our action. But more basically, Kant thinks, moral action is done for the sake of an "independent" or "self-sufficient" end — something already existing, whose value we respect and care about. That end is a *person,* or the *humanity* or *rational nature* in a person or persons.

Kant's term for the special kind of value belonging to that end is: *end in itself* (G 4:427–429). An end in itself is a norm of action for us not because we happen to choose to set it as an end, but because our reason marks out the humanity in persons as having an *objective worth* for whose sake we are morally obligated to act. It is noteworthy that only when we have reached this point in our investigation—that is, when we have both the *form* and the *matter* of the moral principle before us—that Kant regards us as having reached the standpoint of a *metaphysics of morals* (G 4:427). And it is only from the worth of persons as ends in themselves that we can derive positive, general duties we have under the moral principle (G 4:429–430).

Once we have both the form and the matter of the moral principle before us, we can then formulate this principle as the combination of the two, giving us the *complete* statement of the principle. This complete form represents the *idea* of every rational will as giving universal law (G 4:431). The term 'idea' here is crucial. An 'idea' for Kant is a concept formed *a priori* by reason to which no example in experience could ever be adequate. Kant therefore does not hold that our wills, my will or yours, are the actual author or legislator of the moral law. The authority of morality, in his view, is objective, valid in itself for all wills. It does not depend on any legislative will, whether human or divine. But because the human will that truly recognizes and obeys the moral law thereby identifies itself with that law, it can *regard itself* as the legislator of the law and *consider itself* as its author (G 4:431). It therefore may think of the law as legislated to itself by the rational will, or as a law of *autonomy.*

Kant then formulates this idea in a more intuitive way by representing the moral law as the law of an entire community of rational beings, which he calls the *realm of ends (Reich der Zwecke)*. In an ideal community consisting of all rational beings, if all obeyed the moral law, every rational being would be treated by itself and all others as an end in itself; and all the ends they set for themselves would harmonize into a system of shared or collective ends (G 4:433). As a member of this realm of ends, the rational being then acquires, in addition to the value of being an end in itself, also *dignity,* or a value beyond all price, which may not be sacrificed or traded away for anything else (not even something else that has dignity) (G 4:434). Once Kant has derived these three formulas of the moral law from the concept of a categorical imperative, he presents them as a system (G 4:436). Only with this system has Kant's first task in the *Groundwork,* the search for the supreme principle of morality, reached its goal.

Kant tells us later, in the *Critique of Practical Reason,* that when he speaks of different "formulas" of the moral law, he is using this term in a sense similar to its use in mathematics: a "formula" is "that which determines quite precisely what is to be done to solve a problem" (KpV 5:8n). Accordingly, each formula addresses a specific problem and is assigned a function (or a couple of functions). The first formula, the Formula of Universal Law (FUL), and its more intuitive variant, the Formula of the Law of Nature (FLN), have the single function of being the canon or standard of judgment for applying common rational moral cognition to particular cases. Kant's use of them is misunderstood if they are assigned tasks or functions that go beyond that—such as providing a general discursive criterion of right action or moral permissibility. The second formula, The Formula of Humanity as End in Itself (FH), has two functions. First, it provides us with the reason or motive (the sole conceivable one) for obeying a categorical imperative. Second, the interpretation of kinds of conduct in relation to it (conduct which either respects and values humanity or rational nature as end in itself or that fails to do so) allows for the derivation of a set of moral duties. These are exemplified at *Groundwork* 4:429–430 using the same four examples in which FLN applied them as a canon of judgment. The entire system of such duties is presented more completely in the Doctrine of Elements of the Doctrine of Virtue in Kant's *Metaphysics of Morals* (MS 6:415–474).

The combination of FUL/FLN with FH results in the Formula of Autonomy (FA) and its intuitive variant, the Formula of the Realm of Ends (FRE). These formulas solve the problem of providing the most complete and universal formula of the moral law. Because it is the most complete of the formulas, FA also solves a second problem: it is the formula used in the Deduction or "establishment" of the principle in the Third Section of the *Groundwork* (4:447–463).

THIRD SECTION: DEDUCTION OF THE MORAL LAW

Kant's argument in the Third Section is notoriously controversial. Its main elements, however, are clear enough. The argument depends on the presupposition that we are free. He thinks freedom can be neither demonstrated nor even comprehended, but that whenever we judge we must ascribe our judgment to our own reason, acting freely under rational norms, and not necessitated by empirical causes. The moral principle as FA, however, has been identified already as the law pertaining to a free will. Therefore, it must be valid for every rational being. Kant describes this argument as a 'deduction' of the moral principle. He seems to mean this in a sense similar to that used in the Transcendental Deduction of the Categories in the *Critique of Pure Reason*. Its aim is to justify our rightful claim to something of which we already have possession. We already possess both freedom and the moral law that reciprocally implies freedom in the form of our moral consciousness and our awareness of rational agency. We have a rightful claim to these possessions, Kant is arguing, because from a practical point of view we cannot judge or act without presupposing them. Even to doubt that we are free we would have to presuppose that we are free. This provides a deduction or justification of both freedom and the moral law, but only from a practical standpoint. As a theoretical question, freedom of the will remains open; even what it means to be free lies beyond our insight or comprehension. Those who want some positive account of how freedom might be compatible with natural causation are never going to get what they desire.

Kant then raises further questions in the Third Section about whether his argument has involved some kind of circularity. It is also notoriously controversial what this 'circle' is supposed to be and also how Kant proposes to avoid or resolve it. I will not try to address those controversies here. But I will address some common misunderstandings of his argument in the Third Section below under "3. 'Intelligible' freedom."

Some suggestions about how (and how not) to read the *Groundwork*

I have long been of the opinion that the *Groundwork* is very commonly misread on several important points. Sometimes it is misunderstood just as badly by Kant's sympathizers as by his critics. I am fully aware how quixotic it may be of me to try to correct all these misunderstandings in a mere brief introduction to a translation of the work. But it is not at mere windmills that I will be tilting. I am hoping that if readers of my translation are forewarned, some of them may at least be able to keep an open mind about three major issues on which I think most readers of this little book often go wrong.

I. ACTING FROM DUTY AND MORAL WORTH

When Kant says that only actions done from duty have true or authentic moral worth, he is *not criticizing* dutiful actions done in the presence of other incentives—for example, beneficent actions done from inclination such as sympathy or love of honor. On the contrary, he says explicitly that such actions are dutiful, amiable, deserving of praise and encouragement

(G 4:398). His point instead is that only actions to which the agents must constrain themselves out of respect for universal law exhibit that special sort of worth which is most central to morality, and from which, therefore, Kant thinks a formulation of the moral principle can be derived. Kant emphasizes the distinctiveness of the kind of worth he means—its difference from dutifulness, merit, praiseworthiness—by describing it as "true," "authentic," or "inner" moral worth (G 4:397–99). That dutiful actions not done from duty lack this kind of worth does not mean that they are morally inferior to dutiful actions that have this worth. It means only that the agent did not need to exercise rational self-constraint on moral grounds in order to conform the action to duty. That this was unnecessary for the agent does not imply anything negative about the action or the agent. It says only this action does not illustrate the special kind of value that is central to morality, and from which Kant intends to derive his first formula of the moral principle.

Kantian ethics is not hostile to human feelings such as love or sympathetic feeling. Kant regards feeling as indispensable to the motivation of all action, and rational feelings as essential to all moral motivation. Rational feelings include the feeling of respect (G 4:407, 428, 436, 440) and also moral feeling, which, along with love of human beings (*Menschenliebe, philanthropia*). These feelings belong to our rational moral capacities; we could not be rational agents without them (MS 6:399–403). Even empirical feelings, according to Kant, are essential for moral virtue. Kant does not regard Hutchesonian sympathy or moral feeling as the *foundation* of morality; but he does regard it as a moral duty to acquire and cultivate such feelings. Kant's theory of duties includes a duty of sympathetic participation (*Teilnehmung*) (MS 6:456–458). We have a duty, that is, actively to empathize with others and elicit from ourselves feelings of love and sympathy that incite us to help them, both with caring for them and with understanding of their situation. Though they are often overlooked by readers, there are explicit references to this duty in the *Groundwork* itself (G 4:423, 430).

Moreover, in his discussion of "acting from duty," Kant is *not* interested in the "real motive" from which we act in cases where we have more than one incentive for a dutiful action. None of his examples ascribe moral worth to an action where there is both duty and another incentive present and the agent is said to act from duty because the agent chooses duty over this other incentive. I doubt that Kant even thinks agents do, or even can, make such choices between incentives when more than one incentive for the same action is present. As Kant sees it, we choose *actions*. As part of our temperament and character, we have certain incentives for making these choices. But our actions are not *caused* by these incentives. Because we are free agents, our actions are freely chosen, not causally necessitated by anything. If we say that a person is moved by one incentive rather than another in doing this action, then that is a statement about the person's temperament and character, not about the cause of this particular choice.

Kant insists that we have a duty to act from duty. In our judgment of what is morally good, not only should we value conformity to duty but it should also matter whether the action was done for duty's sake (G 4:390; KpV 5:81). But Kant says explicitly that the fulfillment of the duty to act from duty does not consist in performing an "inner action"—that is, the (illusory) act of choosing one incentive over another in a particular case. Instead, we fulfill this duty by assessing our actions correctly—judging them by whether they conform to duty rather than merely whether they satisfy our inclinations or other non-moral ends—and also by striving to be the sort of person in whom duty would be a sufficient incentive for dutiful actions (MS 6:393). This striving is an imperfect or meritorious duty. It is meritorious to strive to be the kind of person who needs no incentive other than duty. In this way, duty should not be a mere "back-up" motive to be called upon when no others are available. Duty should take priority over other incentives, and having a virtuous character consists partly in giving it this priority. But it is not blameworthy to need other incentives to do your duty, as long as you actually do it.

As Kant means the phrase here, to *act from duty* always means to act with "inner necessitation" (or moral self-constraint) in a case where duty will not be done unless through free self-constraint through the thought of the moral law (G 4:400; cf. MS 6:387). But the duty to act from duty is *not* a duty to suppress feelings or inclinations, or even a duty not to act on them when they harmonize with duty.

Related to the duty to act for duty's sake is the temptation to "impurity" (R 6:30). It consists in becoming so *dependent* on other motives to do your duty that you permit your judgments about what your duty is to be warped by these non-moral incentives (G 4:390, 402–405, 423–424; cf. TP 8:279). Kant therefore says it is *hazardous* to let non-moral incentives co-operate with the moral one (KpV 5:72). But even incurring the hazard of corrupt judgment and wrongdoing is not itself wrong if the bad result you are risking never comes about. As we have already seen, Kant devises the Formulas of Universal Law and Law of Nature specifically in order to articulate the principles behind the corrective judgments needed to avoid warping one's moral consciousness through such self-serving deceptions. (For more on this topic, see Wood, 2014, Chapter 1.)

2. THE FORMULAS OF UNIVERSAL LAW AND LAW OF NATURE ARE *ONLY* CANONS OF JUDGMENT

Regarding Kant's use of the formulas of universal law and law of nature (G 4:402, 421): Kant never uses these formulas as general permissibility tests for actions or maxims. He explicitly assigns them only the function of being a "standard" or "canon" of moral *judgment*—that is, a corrective to be used in cases where an agent is tempted by self-love or inclination to *misapply* a concept of duty (G 4:389, 402–405, 411n, 421–425).

These formulas are *not* meant by Kant to provide a general criterion for right action. They are not supposed to be discursive tests for the permissibility of just any policy or maxim that might be brought before them. Some "Kantians" may have made use of FUL or FLN as a "CI-Procedure" for determining the permissibility of maxims. But these formulas are never used in any such way by Kant himself. If you look closely at Kant's actual use of these formulas, you see that the context for which the formulas are designed, and the purpose for which they are used, is always far more limited and specific. The maxims to be tested are always devised by an agent who is tempted to violate a specific duty—a duty which is assumed, and not derivable from these formulas. The agent's maxim attempts to rationalize this possible violation, offering a defense of the thought that the agent should be exempt from the duty in question. But the agent is also conscientious enough to want to present the issue of moral judgment fairly, so the maxim is intended to provide an accurate account of the temptation. It is not a rationalization that might succeed in justifying a similar action, but only for a different agent or in a different case. Further, as we've seen, Kant does not think moral agents *explicitly* employ the reasoning from these formulas in making decisions. The moral agent, he says, "obviously does not think [the formula] abstractly in such a universal form, but actually has [it] always before its eyes and uses [it] as its standard of judgment" (G 4:403–404). Kant's formulas FUL/FLN attempt to articulate philosophically what it is that guides an agent implicitly when the agent shows good judgment in resisting such temptations to make bogus exceptions to specific valid duties (G 4:403–404; cf. 4:423–424). The use of these formulas, as Kant describes it, always presupposes that the agent is aware of a determinate duty. The duties assumed are grounded philosophically, but not on these formulas. Their ground is presented later; they are based on the formula of humanity as end in itself (G 4:429–430).

Kant's ethics recognizes no general decision procedure or criterion of moral right and wrong. *None* of his formulas is supposed to serve this purpose. If many philosophers think that nothing could truly be a "moral principle" unless it does these things, then Kant disagrees with them. (For more on this topic, see Wood, 2017.)

3. "INTELLIGIBLE" FREEDOM

In the Third Section of the *Groundwork,* Kant attempts to "establish" the principle of morality, or to provide a "deduction" of it, through its relation to freedom of the will. He argues that the moral principle, formulated as FA, reciprocally implies that the will subject to it is free. If FA is valid for a will, then that will is a free will; if our will is a free will, then it is subject to FA. Kant does not think we can *prove* that our will is free. But he does think we cannot act, or even judge theoretically, without implicitly *presupposing* that our will is free. This presupposition is not a theoretical proof. It cannot exclude on objective grounds that the freedom we presuppose ourselves to have might be an illusion. We can never *know* that we are free. But the presupposition that we are is one we cannot avoid making whenever we act or even judge—whenever we employ our reason (G 4:447–448). If we do not presuppose we are free, we fall into incoherence.

Kant's basic position about the philosophical problem of free will is that it is insoluble. We cannot avoid presupposing that we are free, but we can neither prove that we are free nor even understand how freedom of the will is possible. In the *Critique of Pure Reason,* Kant argued that we can show that there is no outright contradiction in holding that our actions are free and also subject to natural causality (KrV A538–556/B566–586). He even argues that for practical purposes, we can prove freedom through experience, through the fact that some of our choices, both moral choices and non-moral ones, come about through rational incentives (A802/B830). But as a question of metaphysics, we cannot prove that even these choices are not necessitated by natural causes that would turn our presupposition of freedom into an illusion (A803/B831). From the standpoint of theoretical metaphysics, the freedom we necessarily presuppose in practice remains never more than a logical possibility. That is as far as we can go in defending freedom from a theoretical point of view.

Kant bases this very minimal defense of freedom on the fact that we can think of these actions in two ways, or from two "standpoints": as *phenomena,* subject to natural causality, and as *noumena,* subject to reasons or moral laws (G 4:450–452; cf. KrV A557–558/B585–586). Kant thinks this conceptual distinction constitutes a sufficient reply to those who claim that we contradict ourselves in holding that we are natural beings and also free beings. Our freedom, when we think of ourselves as *intelligible beings* acting according to concepts of reason or understanding, does not contradict the natural determination of our actions, when we think of ourselves as *sensible beings* subject to the causality of the natural world.

The "sensible/intelligible" (or "phenomenal/noumenal") distinction, in relation to freedom, is best thought of merely in the following way: We have *two concepts* of our volitions and actions: one concept is empirical or phenomenal, because we think of these actions as something we both do and observe as part of the natural world, and the other concept is intelligible or noumenal in the sense that we relate these same actions to the moral law and moral duties, our awareness of which comes from our rational faculty rather than from the senses. If it is possible to think the same actions in these two different ways, then it is at least self-consistent (not logically contradictory) to claim that our actions are causally determined (when thought through the sensible or phenomenal concept), but also free (when the very same actions are thought through the intelligible concept). From a theoretical standpoint, the question whether our actions are in fact free may therefore be left open. Then it is settled for us as acting beings not by proof, but by being presupposed as a condition of judgment and choice.

In other words, the distinction between these two concepts of our actions offers us only two *thoughts* that are *logically consistent.* It can never settle *theoretically* the question *how,* or even *whether,* the very same actions can actually be both free and causally determined. There can be no *proof* that we are free and also no proof that we are not. Our freedom can be related to our knowledge of natural causality neither by affirming we are free nor by denying it. Theoretically or metaphysically, we must be skeptics or agnostics about freedom. It's only when we act, or observe human beings behaving as rational agents, that we must presuppose that they are free.

The distinction between ourselves as phenomena and as noumena is misunderstood if it is taken to offer some sort of *supernatural explanation* of freedom, or a positive theory claiming that we are free in some supernatural or noumenal realm, while our empirical actions are all causally determined and therefore not free. We can have no cognition of the supersensible, so such an "explanation" would be unknowable by us. Such a bogus explanation would in any case make no sense of our practical situation, since it is our empirical actions that we must ascribe to ourselves; free actions in a supersensible realm would not be imputable to our empirical selves in this world.

Some scholars have represented the "two standpoints"—looking at ourselves as members of a "world of sense" and a "world of understanding" (G 4:451) as a distinction between the ("third person") perspective of the objective observer and the ("first person") perspective of the agent. But Kant never describes the perspectives in this way, and it too would make no sense. Kant's pragmatic anthropology and philosophy of history presuppose that we *observe* the free actions of human beings (looking at them as free from a "third person" perspective). These inquiries do this by presupposing that we are free and then studying our empirical psychology, social interactions, and the history of our species based on that presupposition (I 8:17, Anth 7:119, 385). The presupposition, as we have seen, is unavoidable for us as agents and subjects of our own judgments, but as a matter of theoretical metaphysics, it cannot be proven, disproven, or in any way comprehended by us.

No *explanation* of freedom, empirical or non-empirical, natural or supernatural, could ever be part of Kant's account. Kant holds that freedom cannot be *explained* at all, or even comprehended. "Freedom can never be comprehended nor . . . can insight into it be gained" (G 4:459). Those *incompatibilist determinists* who deny freedom of the will think we can gain such comprehension and insight—into the fact that freedom is an illusion. Standard *compatibilist* accounts of freedom try to explain how freedom fits into the causal order of nature. They hold that freedom can be comprehended as part of the natural order, that we can gain insight into it. Even supernaturalist *incompatibilist* or *libertarian* theories of freedom offer explanation and comprehension of freedom, and also supposed insight into it, when (for instance) they offer theories of "agent-causation" supposedly exercised by some supernatural or immaterial self.

It is important to see that Kant rejects all three of these kinds of theory, and especially to see that he is just as far from accepting supernaturalist-libertarian theories as naturalist-compatibilist theories. Instead, Kant rejects as unanswerable the very question both these kinds of theory are trying to answer. Kant has *no theory at all* of how freedom relates to natural causality, or of even *how* or *whether* freedom is possible. He holds that *no theoretical argument or theory* enables us to exclude the possibility that freedom is an illusion. In that sense, Kant is perhaps closer to the incompatibilist-determinists than to either the naturalist-compatibilists or the supernaturalist-libertarians. But of course he also rejects—not as demonstrably false but merely as forever theoretically undecidable—the proposition that freedom and natural determinism are incompatible.

The result of Kant's reflections on the metaphysical problem of free will is surely unwelcome news for metaphysicians—both naturalist and supernaturalist. It is probably unwelcome even for common sense, which recoils in horror at the thought that something so intimately bound up with our every thought and action is at the same time so utterly alien and incomprehensible to us. The main impulse behind *compatibilist* theories of freedom is surely the comforting thought that there must be some easy and obvious way to make the problem of freedom *just go away*. It is surely unnerving to common sense to be told that freedom is practically *undeniable*—but also theoretically *incomprehensible*.

Those who find this Kantian message too disorienting may think they can make sense of it only by ascribing to Kant some sort of positive theory of freedom, however weird or outlandish. I think that's why they sometimes associate with Kant a transcendent metaphysics of noumenal selves floating about like ectoplasmic jellyfish in a celestial sea beyond space and time, where our supposedly free acts could of course have no conceivable human context or meaning. Critics who interpret Kant this way therefore sometimes hasten to point out—thinking they are refuting Kant—that these purely noumenal or intelligible actions outside space and time could not properly speaking be free acts at all. An absurd theory, easily ridiculed and dismissed, is far easier to deal with than the disconcerting message that we are forever condemned to frustration when we try to think about our freedom as a question of theoretical metaphysics. But when people ascribe to Kant a crazy metaphysical theory of supernatural noumenal selves, they are merely punishing the messenger while depriving themselves of the message.

Kant's whole critical philosophy—its account of the "peculiar fate" of our human predicament—is really about the conveying of this same unwelcome and deeply disorienting message: There are certain questions we are driven to ask by the very nature of our reason itself, but which we can never answer, or even fully understand (KrV Avii). The most we can do is understand why we need to ask these questions, come to see why we cannot even make sense of them, and then—if we are wise—come reluctantly to accept the fact of our inevitable perplexity and frustration. Kant's critical philosophy treats many of the questions of traditional metaphysics as falling under this unwelcome heading. The possibility of human freedom is perhaps the deepest and most disturbing of all these questions. (For more on this topic, see Wood, 2008, Chapter 7.)

The *Groundwork* is morality and also philosophy

Kant's *Groundwork* appears to begin with something like "moral common sense," but it does so already at a lofty philosophical level, removed from common life. It invites us to consider the arresting proposition: "There is nothing it is possible to think of anywhere in the world, or indeed anything at all outside it, that can be held to be good without limitation, excepting only a **good will**" (G 4:393). Along the way it introduces us to moral ideas that have since been the source of much inspiration: That all human beings are ends in themselves, beings with dignity or incomparable worth; that it is our vocation in this life to be autonomous or self-governing beings; that we even constitute an ideal community united by ends that are the ends of all of us; they harmonize into a single system of ends we all can and should share. These are ideas that can generate warmth and enthusiasm, as we come to recognize them as the source of much moral inspiration in modern culture.

But Kant's short book always argues at a highly abstract philosophical level. We must never lose sight of the fact that its sole concern is with the formulation of the supreme principle of morality. Anything more concrete or tangible than that is always being put in service of this task—whether by way of argument or as illustration of the dizzying abstractions with which Kant is in the end exclusively concerned. The argument takes us far from the warmth of everyday feeling and moral inspiration, ending in the iciest of all regions of the moral intellect: "The uttermost boundary of all practical philosophy" (G 4:455). This is the dark, cold uncanny region of thought where we must confront the fact that we cannot comprehend even the possibility of a categorical imperative—of the principle which has been the sole topic of the treatise. We must instead feel lucky if we can even "comprehend its *incomprehensibility*" (G 4:463).

A reader of the *Groundwork* must approach it with no illusions about the chilling and dizzying effect on us that Kant fully realized its argument might have. But the absolute zero frigidity, obscurity, and disorientation should not be seen as part of the morality itself whose ground Kant is attempting to lay. As an everyday moralist, Kant is no enemy of human warmth or feeling. He is in that respect as much an eighteenth-century moralist as Jean-Jacques Rousseau, or David Hume, or Adam Smith. Kant takes seriously the common-sense conceptions of moral virtue and duty, and he means to give expression to our caring for others, our respect for them, and also for ourselves that everyday morality is supposed to involve. But Kant is also first and foremost a philosopher whose primary concern is to discover the foundations of the values and concerns represented by moral common sense. The forbidding features of Kant's critical enterprise are bound to attach to the philosophical foundations of anything that goes as deep into human existence as morality does. Only a reader who is willing to explore the foundations of moral philosophy, just as a traveler might visit the coldest and most remote regions of our solar system, can expect to return from the journey with genuine understanding of the challenging thoughts that make the contents of this little book such a powerful influence on all moral philosophy since its first publication over twenty-three decades ago.

A Note on the Translation

Kant's *Grundlegung zur Metaphysik der Sitten* has had many English translations. The most estimable, in my opinion, are those by Thomas K. Abbott (1883), H. J. Paton (1948), Lewis White Beck (1949; revised several times, most notably in 1959 and 1990), and Mary J. Gregor (1996). Yet I came to find even these translations unsatisfying at certain points because they are too often content to remain at a distance from what Kant actually said in order to provide the reader with smoother English, and they sometimes commit themselves too much to one possible interpretation where the original text is tantalizingly ambiguous.

In the present translation my aim has been to place the English reader, as far as possible, in the same interpretive position as the German reader of the original. It is not always possible to do this, but it is always undesirable not to, even when you provide an interpretation that is more correct than its possible alternatives. My principle is that a translator has one task, an interpreter a different task. In my introduction, if you have read it, you've seen me being an *interpreter* of the *Groundwork*. From here on, however, *you* are supposed to be the interpreter. I am trying to function only as a *translator*. My sole obligation from this point on is to present Kant's German text to you in English as well as I can. Where Kant's writing is obscure or awkward, I have tried to reproduce the same murkiness and cumbersomeness in English that the German reader would encounter. It is now *your* job—no doubt with the help of other interpreters, such as those listed in the Select Bibliography—to figure out what it means.

Some people say, correctly, that in translating, some interpretation is unavoidable. They sometimes put it sententiously: "Every translation is an interpretation"; then they conclude that translators should feel entitled, or even obligated, to impose their interpretation of a text on the reader in translating the text. My reply to this line of thinking is: We also cannot completely eliminate child molestation. But we should try, and we certainly should not encourage it.

These rules of translation have dictated taking pains to achieve accuracy and literalness, as far as this can be made consistent with intelligibility. It has also led to the attempt to preserve, as far as possible, a consistency in terminology, not only with technical terms but even with non-technical ones. Otherwise, the priorities in translating any text must obviously depend on the nature and purpose of the text itself. Poetry should probably be translated only by poets; philosophy certainly needs to be translated by philosophers. What matters in a philosophical text is almost exclusively *what it means*. How it is said sometimes also matters, but far less in a philosophical writer such as Kant than in one such as Plato, Augustine, Anselm, Descartes, Pascal, or Nietzsche. What a philosophical text means is constituted by the range of possible alternative constructions that a reader's philosophical imagination can justifiably put on the words in which the text expresses its questions, doctrines, and arguments. The translation of a work like this one succeeds, therefore, to the extent that it provides a reliable basis for this work of imagination, neither constraining the reader to adopt the translator's own preferred imaginings nor suggesting possible meanings that the original text cannot bear.

The first edition of this translation was published in 2002 as part of the Yale University Press Rethinking the Western Tradition series. It included critical essays by J. B. Schneewind, Marcia Baron, Shelly Kagan, and myself. A direct incitement to do a new translation of the *Groundwork* at that time was the availability of the new edition of the German text, published by Bernd Kraft and Dieter Schönecker in the Philosophische Bibliothek series, Felix Meiner Verlag. This text of the *Grundlegung* was used as the basis for the present translation. One of the special virtues of the new Meiner Verlag edition is its attention to variations between the two earliest versions of the text, the first published in 1785, the second a year later. The edition usually follows the 1786 version, but notes inform the reader of the differences. The present translation does likewise wherever textual differences make a difference in translation (which they usually do). In a few places, I have also followed the editors of the new text in making textual emendations where the sense seems to require it. But I did this only reluctantly (and less often than the editors of the original text did); wherever emendations are made, of course, a footnote informs the reader; in some cases, a note suggests a possible emendation, and what it would have meant in the translation, but without actually adopting it.

This translation has benefited greatly from careful comments by, and long discussions with, Dieter Schönecker. His care, precision, and linguistic expertise, and even more his intimate knowledge of the text of the

Grundlegung, saved me from many errors and led to many improvements in the translation. Schönecker and Kraft also made available to me a draft of their editorial notes; I tried to reciprocate this favor by providing them with some informational notes they did not yet have. Also helpful were textual corrections and thoughtful stylistic suggestions made by Derek Parfit. In identifying Kant's references to classical philosophy and literature, I also benefited from the expertise, erudition, and generosity of Rega Wood, Tad Brennan, John Cooper, and Elizabeth Tylawsky.

Over the years, I have become aware of some errors in it, and also some things I now prefer to do slightly differently. I am indebted to Dieter Schönecker for several corrections. I don't suppose that this translation, or any work of mine of any kind, will ever be perfect. But I think this second edition of the translation is at least improved over the first edition. I hope that in this translation I have presented Kant's *Groundwork* in a way that will further its ongoing appropriation by everyone who thinks about the fundamental issues raised in it.

Groundwork
for
the Metaphysics of Morals

[Ak 4:385]

IMMANUEL KANT

Preface

Ancient Greek philosophy partitioned itself into three sciences: **physics, ethics,** and **logic.**[1] This division is perfectly suitable to the nature of the thing and one cannot improve upon it, except only by adding its principle, in order in this way partly to secure its completeness and partly to be able to determine correctly the necessary subdivisions.

All rational cognition is either *material,* and considers some object, or *formal,* and concerns itself merely with the form of the understanding and of reason itself and the universal rules of thinking in general, without distinction among objects.[2] Formal philosophy is called **logic,** but material philosophy, which has to do with determinate objects and the laws to which they are subjected, is once again twofold. For these laws are either laws of **nature** or of **freedom.** The science of the first is called **physics,** and that of the other is **ethics;** the former is also named 'doctrine of nature', the latter 'doctrine of morals'.

Logic can have no empirical part, i.e., a part such that the universal and necessary laws of thinking rest on grounds that are taken from experience; for otherwise it would not be logic, i.e., a canon for the understanding or reason which is valid for all thinking and must be demonstrated. By contrast, natural and moral philosophy can each have their empirical part, because the former must determine its laws of nature as an object of experience, the latter must determine the laws for the will of the human being insofar as he is affected by nature—the first as laws in accordance with which everything happens, the second as those in accordance with which everything ought to happen, but also reckoning with the conditions under which it often does not happen.

One can call all philosophy, insofar as it is based on grounds of experience, *empirical,* but that which puts forth its doctrines solely from principles *a priori, pure* philosophy. The latter, when it is merely formal, is called *logic;* but if it is limited to determinate objects of the understanding, then[a] it is called *metaphysics.*

In such a wise there arises the idea of a twofold metaphysics, the idea of a *metaphysics of nature* and of a *metaphysics of morals.* Physics will thus have its empirical but also a rational part; and ethics likewise; although here the empirical part in particular could be called *practical anthropology,* but the rational part could properly be called *morals.*[b]

All trades, handicrafts, and arts have gained through the division of labor, since, namely, one person does not do everything, but rather each limits himself to a certain labor which distinguishes itself markedly from others by its manner of treatment, in order to be able to perform it in the greatest perfection and with more facility. Where labors are not so distinguished and divided, where each is a jack-of-all-trades, there the trades still remain in the greatest barbarism. But it might be a not unworthy object of consideration to ask whether pure philosophy in all its parts does not require each its particular man, and whether it would not stand better with the learned trade as a whole if those who, catering to the taste of the public, are accustomed to sell the empirical along with the rational, mixed in all sorts of proportions[c] unknown even to themselves—calling themselves 'independent thinkers',[d] and those who prepare the merely rational part 'quibblers'[e]—if they were warned not to carry on simultaneously two enterprises that are very different in their mode of treatment, each of which perhaps requires a particular talent, and the combination of which in a single person produces only bunglers: thus I here ask only whether the nature of the science does not require the empirical part always to be carefully separated from the rational, placing ahead of a genuine (empirical) physics a metaphysics of nature, and ahead of practical anthropology a metaphysics of morals, which must be carefully cleansed of everything empirical, in order to know how much pure reason could achieve in both cases; and

[Ak 4:389] from these sources pure reason itself creates its teachings *a priori,* whether the latter enterprise be carried on by all teachers of morals (whose name is legion) or only by some who feel they have a calling for it.

a. 1785: "..., is called ..."
b. Kant later includes "principles of application" drawn from "the particular nature of human beings" *within* "metaphysics of morals" itself, leaving "practical anthropology" to deal "only with the subjective conditions in human nature that hinder people or help them in fulfilling the laws of a metaphysics of morals" (MS 6:217).
c. *Verhältnisse*
d. *Selbstdenker*
e. *Grübler*

Since my aim here is properly directed to moral philosophy, I limit the proposed question only to this: whether one is not of the opinion that it is of the utmost necessity to work out once a pure moral philosophy which is fully cleansed of everything that might be in any way empirical and belong to anthropology; for that there must be such is self-evident from the common idea of duty and of moral laws. Everyone must admit that a law, if it is to be valid morally, i.e. as the ground of an obligation, has to carry absolute necessity with it; that the command "You ought not lie" is valid not merely for human beings, as though other rational beings did not have to heed it; and likewise all the other genuinely moral laws; hence that the ground of obligation here is to be sought not in the nature of the human being or the circumstances of the world in which he is placed, but *a priori* solely in concepts of pure reason, and that every other precept grounded on principles of mere experience, and even a precept that is universal in a certain aspect, insofar as it is supported in the smallest part on empirical grounds, perhaps only as to its motive, can be called a practical rule, but never a moral law.

Thus not only are moral laws together with their principles essentially distinguished among all practical cognition from everything else in which there is anything empirical, but all moral philosophy rests entirely on its pure part, and when applied to the human being it borrows not the least bit from knowledge about him (anthropology), but it gives him as a rational being laws *a priori,* which to be sure require a power of judgment sharpened through experience, partly to distinguish in which cases they have their application, and partly to obtain access for them to the will of the human being and emphasis for their fulfillment, since he,[a] as affected with so many inclinations, is susceptible to the idea of a pure practical reason, but is not so easily capable of making it effective *in concreto* in his course of life.

Thus a metaphysics of morals is indispensably necessary not merely from a motive of speculation, in order to investigate the source of the [Ak 4:390] practical principles lying *a priori* in our reason, but also because morals themselves remain subject to all sorts of corruption as long as that guiding thread and supreme norm of their correct judgment is lacking. For as to what is to be morally good, it is not enough that it *conform* to the moral law, but it must also happen *for the sake of this law;* otherwise, that conformity is only contingent and precarious, because the unmoral ground

a. Kant's text reads *diese,* which would refer to 'fulfillment'; editors suggest amending it to *dieser.*

will now and then produce lawful actions, but more often actions contrary to the law. But now the moral law in its purity and genuineness (which is precisely what most matters in the practical) is to be sought nowhere else than in a pure philosophy; hence this (metaphysics) must go first, and without it there can be no moral philosophy at all; that which mixes those pure principles among empirical ones does not even deserve the name of a 'philosophy' (for this distinguishes itself from common rational cognition precisely by the fact that what the latter conceives only as mixed in, it expounds in a separate science), still less of a 'moral philosophy', because precisely through this mixture it violates the purity of morals and proceeds contrary to its own end.

One should not think that what is here demanded we already have in the propaedeutic of the famous *Wolff* in his moral philosophy, namely in what he calls *universal practical philosophy,*[3] and thus that here an entirely new field is not to be entered on. Precisely because it is supposed to be a universal practical philosophy, it has not drawn into consideration any will of a particular kind, such as one determined without any empirical motives fully from principles *a priori,* which one could call a 'pure will', but only volition in general, with all actions and conditions that pertain to it in this universal signification; and thereby it is distinguished from a metaphysics of morals just as general logic is from transcendental philosophy, of which the first expounds the actions and rules of thinking *in general,* but the latter merely the particular actions and rules of **pure** thinking, i.e. those through which objects can be cognized fully *a priori.* For the metaphysics of morals is to investigate the idea and principles of a possible *pure* will, and not the actions and conditions of human volition in general, which are for the most part drawn from psychology. It constitutes no objection to my assertion that moral laws and duty are also discussed in universal practical philosophy (though contrary to all warrant). For in this too the authors of that science remain faithful to their idea of it; they do not distinguish the motives that are represented as such fully *a priori* merely through reason, and are properly moral, from the empirical ones which understanding raises to universal concepts through the comparison of experiences; but rather they consider them, without respecting the distinction of their sources, only in accordance with their greater or smaller sum (since they are all regarded as homogeneous), and through that they make for themselves their concept of *obligation,* which is to be sure not less than moral, but is so constituted as can be demanded only in a philosophy that does not judge about the *origin* of all practical concepts, whether they occur *a priori* or merely *a posteriori.*

[Ak 4:391]

Now intending someday to provide a metaphysics of morals, I issue this groundwork in advance.[4] There is, to be sure, really no other foundation for it than the critique of a *pure practical reason,* just as for metaphysics there is the already provided critique of pure speculative reason. Yet in part the former is not of such utmost necessity as the latter, because in what is moral human reason, even in the most common understanding, can easily be brought to great correctness and completeness, whereas in its theoretical but pure use it is entirely dialectical; in part I require for a critique of a pure practical reason that if it is to be completed, its unity with the[a] speculative in a common principle must at the same time be exhibited, because it can in the end be only one and the same reason that is distinguished merely in its application. But I could not bring it to such a completeness here without bringing in considerations of an entirely different kind and confusing the reader. It is for the sake of this that instead of the term *Critique of pure practical reason* I have used instead *Groundwork for the metaphysics of morals.*[5]

But, thirdly, because a metaphysics of morals, despite its intimidating title, is yet susceptible to a high degree of popularity and suitability to the common understanding, I find it useful to separate from it this preliminary work of laying the ground, in order that in the future I need not attach subtleties, which are unavoidable in it, to more easily grasped doctrines.   [Ak 4:392]

The present groundwork is, however, nothing more than the search for and establishment *of the supreme principle of morality,* which already constitutes an enterprise whole in its aim and to be separated from every other moral investigation. To be sure, my assertions about this important and principal question, whose discussion has hitherto been far from satisfactory, would receive much light through the application of the same principle to the entire system, and of confirmation through the adequacy it manifests everywhere; yet I had to dispense with this advantage, which would also be basically more a matter of my self-love than of the common utility, because the facility of use and the apparent adequacy of a principle provide no wholly secure proof of its correctness, but rather awaken a certain partiality not to investigate and consider it for itself without any regard for the consequences.

The method I have taken in this work, I believe, is the one best suited if one wants to take the way analytically from common cognition to the determination of its supreme principle and then, in turn, synthetically from

---

a. In 1785 this definite article *der* is repeated; that version would be translated: ". . . its unity with the critique of speculative reason in a common principle . . ."

the testing of this principle and its sources back to common cognition, in which its use is encountered. Hence the division turns out thus:

1. *First section:* Transition from common rational moral cognition to philosophical moral cognition.
2. *Second section:* Transition from popular moral philosophy to the metaphysics of morals.
3. *Third section:* Final step from the metaphysics of morals to the critique of pure practical reason.

First section

Transition
from common rational moral cognition
to philosophical moral cognition

There is nothing it is possible to think of anywhere in the world, or indeed anything at all outside it, that can be held to be good without limitation, excepting only a **good will**. Understanding, wit, the power of judgment[1] and like *talents* of the mind,[a] whatever they might be called, or courage, resoluteness, persistence in an intention, as qualities of *temperament*, are without doubt in some respects good and to be wished for; but they can also become extremely evil and harmful if the will that is to make use of these gifts of nature, and whose peculiar constitution is therefore called *character*,[2] is not good. It is the same with *gifts of fortune*. Power, wealth, honor,[3] even health and that entire well-being and contentment with one's condition, under the name of *happiness*, make for courage and thereby often also for audacity,[b] where there is not a good will to correct their influence on the mind,[c] and thereby on the entire principle of action, and make them universally purposive;[d] not to mention that a rational impartial spectator[4] can never take satisfaction even in the sight of the uninterrupted welfare of a being, if it is adorned with no trait of a pure and good will; and so the good will appears to constitute the indispensable condition even of the worthiness to be happy.

Some qualities are even conducive to this good will itself and can make its work much easier, but still have despite this no inner unconditioned worth, yet always presuppose a good will, which limits the esteem[e] which one otherwise rightly has for them, and does not permit them to be held absolutely good. Moderation in affects and passions,[5] self-control and sober reflection are not only good for many aims, but seem even to constitute a part of the *inner* worth of a person; yet they lack much in order to

a. *Geist*
b. *Mut und hierdurch öfters auch Übermut*
c. *Gemüt*
d. *allgemein-zweckmäßig*, which could also be translated as 'generally suitable'
e. 1786 reads *Hochschätzung;* 1785 reads *Schätzung* ('estimation')

be declared good without limitation (however unconditionally they were praised by the ancients).[6] For without the principles of a good will they can become extremely evil, and the cold-bloodedness of a villain makes him not only far more dangerous but also immediately more abominable in our eyes than he would have been held without it.

The good will is good not through what it effects or accomplishes, not through its serviceability for the attainment of any intended end, but only through its willing, i.e. good in itself, and considered for itself, without comparison, it is to be estimated far higher than anything that could be brought about by it in favor of any inclination, or indeed, if you prefer, of the sum of all inclinations. Even if through the peculiar disfavor of fate, or through the meager endowment of a stepmotherly nature, this will were entirely lacking in the resources to carry out its aim, if with its greatest effort nothing were accomplished by it, and only the good will were left over (to be sure, not a mere wish, but as the mobilization of all means insofar as they are in our control): then it would shine all by itself[a] like a jewel, as something that has its full worth in itself. Utility or fruitlessness can neither add to nor subtract anything from this worth. It would be only the setting, as it were, to make it easier to handle in common traffic, or to draw the attention of those who are still not sufficiently connoisseurs; but not to recommend it to connoisseurs and determine its worth.

There is, however, something so strange in this idea of the absolute worth of the mere will, without making any allowance for utility in its estimation, that despite all the agreement with it even of common reason, there must nevertheless arise a suspicion that perhaps it is covertly grounded merely on a high-flown fantasy, and that nature might have been falsely [Ak 4:395] understood in the aim it had in assigning reason to govern our will. Hence we will put this idea to the test from this point of view.

In the natural predispositions of an organized being, i.e. a being arranged purposively[b] for life, we assume as a principle that no instrument is to be encountered in it for any end except that which is the most suitable to and appropriate for it.[7] Now if, in a being that has reason and a will, its *preservation,* its *welfare*—in a word, its *happiness*—were the real end of nature, then nature would have hit on a very bad arrangement in appointing reason in this creature to accomplish the aim. For all the actions it has to execute toward this aim, and the entire rule of its conduct, would be prescribed to it much more precisely through instinct, and that end could be

a. *für sich*
b. *zweckmäßig,* which could also be translated 'suitably'

obtained far more safely through it than could ever happen through reason; and if, over and above this, reason were imparted to the favored creature, it would have served it only to make it consider the happy predisposition of its nature, to admire it, rejoice in it, and to make it grateful to the beneficent cause of it, but not to subject its faculty of desire to that weak and deceptive guidance, and meddle in the aim of nature; in a word, nature would have prevented reason from breaking out into *practical use* and from having the presumption, with its weak insight, to think out for itself the project of happiness and the means of attaining it; nature would have taken over not only the choice of the ends but also of the means, and with wise provision would have entrusted both solely to instinct.⁸

In fact we also find that the more a cultivated reason gives itself over to the aim of enjoying life and happiness, the farther the human being falls short of true contentment; from this arises in many, and indeed in those most practiced in the cultivated use of reason, if only they are sincere enough to admit it, a certain degree of *misology,* i.e. hatred of reason;⁹ for after reckoning all the advantages they draw, I do not say from the invention of all the arts of common luxury,¹⁰ but even from the sciences (which also seem to them in the end to beᵃ a luxury of the understanding), they nevertheless find that they have in fact only brought moreᵇ hardship down on their shoulders than they have gained in happiness, and on this account in the end they sooner envy than despise human beings of the more common stamp, who are closer to the guidance of mere natural instinct and do not permit their reason much influence over their conduct.ᶜ And we must admit this much, that the judgment of those who very much moderate the boastful high praise of the advantages that reason is supposed to supply us in regard to happiness and contentment with life, or who even reduce it below zero, is by no means morose or ungrateful toward the kindness of the world's government; but rather these judgments are covertly grounded on the idea of another aim for their existence, possessing much greater dignity, for which, and not for their happiness, reason has been given its wholly authentic vocation, and to which, therefore, as a supreme condition, the private aims of the human being must for the most part defer.

[Ak 4:396]

For since reason is not sufficiently effective in guiding the will safely in regard to its objects and the satisfaction of all our needs (which it in part

---

a. 1785 reads *scheint* instead of *zu sein scheinen,* which would have the effect in translation of eliminating the words "to be" from this sentence.

b. 1785: "more of"

c. *Tun und Lassen*

itself multiplies), and an implanted natural instinct would have guided us much more certainly to this end, yet since reason nevertheless has been imparted to us as a practical faculty, i.e. as one that ought to have influence on the *will,* its true vocation must therefore be not to produce volition *as a means* to some other aim, but rather to produce a *will good in itself,* for which reason was absolutely necessary, since everywhere else nature goes to work purposively[a] in distributing its predispositions. This will may therefore not be the single and entire good, but it must be the highest good, and the condition for all the rest, even for every demand for happiness, in which case it can be united with the wisdom of nature, when one perceives that the culture of reason, which is required for the former, limits in many ways the attainment of the second aim, which is always conditioned, namely of happiness, at least in this life, and can even diminish it to less than nothing without nature's proceeding unpurposively[b] in this; for reason, which recognizes its highest practical vocation in the grounding of a good will, is capable in attaining this aim only of a contentment after its own kind, namely from the fulfillment of an[c] end that again only reason determines, even if this should also be bound up with some infringement of the ends of inclination.

[Ak 4:397]   But now in order to develop the concept of a good will, to be esteemed in itself and without any further aim, just as it dwells already[d] in the naturally healthy understanding, which does not need to be taught but rather only to be enlightened, this concept always standing over the estimation of the entire worth of our actions and constituting the condition for everything else: we will put before ourselves the concept of *duty,* which contains that of a good will, although under certain subjective limitations and hindrances, which, however, far from concealing it and making it unrecognizable, rather elevate it by contrast and let it shine forth all the more brightly.

I pass over all actions that are already recognized as contrary to duty, even though they might be useful for this or that aim; for with them the question cannot arise at all whether they might be done *from duty,* since they even conflict with it. I also set aside the actions which are actually in conformity with duty, for which, however, human beings have immediately *no inclination,* but nevertheless perform them because they are driven to it

a. *zweckmäßig*
b. *unzweckmäßig,* which could also mean: unsuitably, uncomfortably, or pointlessly
c. 1785: "of the end"
d. This word added in 1786

through another inclination. For there it is easy to distinguish whether the action in conformity with duty is done *from duty* or from a self-seeking aim. It is much harder to notice this difference where the action is in conformity with duty and the subject yet has beside this an *immediate* inclination to it. E.g., it is indeed in conformity with duty that the shopkeeper should not overcharge his inexperienced customers, and where there is much commercial traffic, the prudent merchant also does not do this, but rather holds a firm general price for everyone, so that a child buys just as cheaply from him as anyone else. Thus one is *honestly* served; yet that is by no means sufficient for us to believe that the merchant has proceeded thus from duty and from principles of honesty; his advantage required it; but here it is not to be assumed that beside this, he was also supposed to have an immediate inclination toward the customers, so that out of love, as it were, he gave no one an advantage over another in his prices. Thus the action was done neither from duty nor from immediate inclination, but merely from a self-serving aim.

By contrast, to preserve one's life is a duty, and beside this everyone has an immediate inclination to it. But the often anxious care that the greatest part of humankind takes for its sake still has no inner worth, and its maxim has no moral content. They protect their life, to be sure, *in conformity with* [Ak 4:398] *duty*, but not *from duty*. If, by contrast, adversities and hopeless grief have entirely taken away the taste for life, if the unhappy one, strong of soul, more indignant than pusillanimous or dejected over his fate, wishes for death and yet preserves his life without loving it, not from inclination or fear, but from duty: then his maxim has a moral content.

To be beneficent where one can is a duty, and beside this there are some souls so attuned to sympathetic participation[a] that even without any other motive of vanity or utility to self, they take an inner gratification in spreading joy around them, and can take delight in the contentment of others insofar as it is their own work. But I assert that in such a case the action, however it may conform to duty and however amiable it is, nevertheless has no true moral worth, but is on the same footing as other inclinations, e.g. the inclination to honor, which, when it fortunately encounters something that in fact serves the common good and is in conformity with duty, and is thus worthy of honor, deserves praise and encouragement, but not esteem; for the maxim lacks moral content, namely of doing such actions not from inclination but *from duty*. Thus suppose the mind of that same

a. *teilnehmend gestimmte Seelen*

friend of humanity were clouded over with his own grief, extinguishing all his sympathetic participation[a] in the fate of others; he still has the resources to be beneficent to those suffering distress, but the distress[b] of others does not touch him because he is[c] sufficiently busy with his own; and now, where no inclination any longer stimulates him to it, he tears himself out of this deadly insensibility and does the action without any inclination, solely from duty; only then does it for the first time have its authentic moral worth. Even more: if nature had put little sympathy[d] at all in the heart of this or that person, if he (an honest man, to be sure) were by temperament cold and indifferent toward the sufferings of others, perhaps because he himself is provided with particular gifts of patience and strength to endure his own, and also presupposes or even demands the same of others; if nature has not really formed[e] such a man into a friend of humanity (though he would not in truth be its worst product), nevertheless would he not find a source within himself to give himself a far higher worth than that which a good-natured temperament might have? By all means! Just here begins the worth of character, which is moral and the highest without any comparison, namely that he is beneficent not from inclination but from duty.

[Ak 4:399]

To secure one's own happiness is a duty (at least indirectly), for the lack of contentment with one's condition, in a crowd of many sorrows and amid unsatisfied needs, can easily become a great *temptation to the violation of duties*. But even without looking at duty, all human beings always have of themselves the most powerful and inward inclination to happiness, because precisely in this idea all inclinations are united in a sum. Yet the precept of happiness is for the most part so constituted that it greatly infringes on some inclinations and yet the human being cannot make any determinate and secure concept of the sum of satisfaction of them all, under the name of 'happiness'; hence it is not to be wondered at that a single inclination, which is determinate in regard to what it promises and the time in which its satisfaction can be obtained, can outweigh a wavering idea; and the human being, e.g. a person with gout, could choose to enjoy what tastes good and to suffer what he must, because in accordance with his reckoning, here at least he has not sacrificed the enjoyment of the present moment through expectations, perhaps groundless, of a happiness that is supposed to lie in health. But also in this case, if the general inclination to happiness does not

a. *Teilnehmung*
b. *Not*
c. 1785 puts this word in the subjunctive (*wäre*).
d. *Sympathie*
e. *gebildet*

determine his will, if for him, at least, health does not count as so necessary in his reckoning, then here as in all other cases, there still remains a law, namely to promote his happiness not from inclination but from duty, and then his conduct has for the first time its authentic moral worth.

It is in this way, without doubt, that those passages in scripture are to be understood in which it is commanded to love our neighbor and even our enemy. For love as inclination cannot be commanded; but beneficence solely from duty, even when no inclination at all drives us to it, or even when natural and invincible disinclination resists, is *practical* and not *pathological* love, which lies in the will and not in the propensity of feeling, in the principles of action and not in melting sympathy;[a] but the former alone can be commanded.

The second proposition[11] is: an action from duty has its moral worth *not in the aim* that is supposed to be attained by it, but rather in the maxim in accordance with which it is resolved upon; thus[b] that worth depends not on the actuality of the object of the action, but merely on the *principle of the volition,* in accordance with which the action is done, without regard to any object of the faculty of desire. It is clear from the preceding that the aims we may have in actions, and their effects, as ends and incentives of the will, can impart to the actions no unconditioned and moral worth. In what, then, can this worth lie, if it is not supposed to exist in the will, in the relation of the actions to the effect hoped for? It can lie nowhere else *than in the principle of the will,* without regard to the ends that can be effected through such action; for the will is at a parting of the ways,[c] as it were, between its principle *a priori,* which is formal, and its incentive *a posteriori,* which is material, and since it must somehow be determined by something, it must be determined through the formal principle in general of the volition if it does an action from duty, since every material principle has been withdrawn from it. [Ak 4:400]

The third proposition, as a consequence of the first two, I would express thus: *Duty is the necessity of an action from respect for the law.* For the object, as an effect of my proposed action, I can of course have an *inclination,* but *never respect,* just because it[d] is merely an effect and not the activity of a will.[e] Just as little can I have respect for inclination in general, whether

---

a. *schmelzender Teilnehmung*

b. This last clause, absent from 1785, was added in 1786.

c. *Scheideweg*

d. Kant's pronoun here is in the feminine, which could refer to 'effect' but not to 'object'. Editors therefore often emend the pronoun to the neuter.

e. 1785 reads: "an effect of my will"

my own or another's; I can at most approve it in the first case, in the second I can sometimes even love it, i.e. regard it as favorable to my own advantage. Only that which is connected with my will merely as a ground, never as an effect, only what does not serve my inclination but outweighs it, or at least wholly excludes it from the reckoning in a choice, hence only the mere law for itself, can be an object of respect and hence a command. Now an action from duty is supposed entirely to abstract from[a] the influence of inclination, and with it every object of the will, so nothing is left over for the will that can determine it except the *law* as what is objective and subjectively *pure respect* for this practical law, hence the maxim* of complying with such a law, even when it infringes all my inclinations.

[Ak 4:401]

The moral worth of the action thus lies not in the effect to be expected from it; thus also not in any principle of action which needs to get its motive from this expected effect. For all these effects (agreeableness of one's condition, indeed even the furthering of the happiness of others) could be brought about through other causes, and for them the will of a rational being is therefore not needed; but in it alone the highest and unconditioned good can nevertheless be encountered. Nothing other than the *representation of the law* in itself, *which obviously occurs only in the rational being* insofar as it, and not the hoped for effect, is the determining ground of the will, therefore[b] constitutes that so pre-eminent good which we call 'moral', which is already present in the person himself who acts in accordance with it, but must not first of all be expected from the effect.[†]

a. *absondern*

[Ak 4:401]

*A *maxim* is the subjective principle of the volition; the objective principle (i.e., that which would serve all rational beings also subjectively as a practical principle if reason had full control over the faculty of desire) is the practical *law*.

b. 1785 reads: "thus"

[Ak 4:402]

[†]One could accuse me of merely taking refuge behind the word *respect* in an obscure feeling instead of giving distinct information through a concept of reason. Yet even if respect is a feeling, it is not one *received* through influence but a feeling *self-effected* through a concept of reason and hence specifically distinguished from all feelings of the first kind, that may be reduced to inclination or fear. What I immediately recognize as a law for me, I recognize with respect, which signifies merely the consciousness of the *subjection* of my will to a law without any mediation of other influences on my sense. The immediate determination of the will through the law and the consciousness of it is called *respect,* so that the latter is to be regarded as the *effect* of the law on the subject and not as its *cause.* Authentically, respect is the representation of a worth that infringes on my self-love. Thus it is something that is considered neither as an object of inclination nor of fear, even though it has something analogical to both at the same time. The *object* of respect is thus solely the law, and specifically that law that we *lay upon ourselves*

But what kind of law can it be, whose representation, without even [Ak 4:402] taking account of the effect expected from it, must determine the will, so that it can be called good absolutely and without limitation? Since I have robbed the will of every impulse that could have arisen from the obedience to any law, there is nothing left over except the universal lawfulness of the action in general which alone is to serve the will as its principle, i.e. I ought never to conduct myself except so *that I could also will that my maxim become a universal law.* Here it is mere lawfulness in general (without grounding it on any law determining certain actions) that serves the will as its principle, and also must so serve it, if duty is not to be everywhere an empty delusion and a chimerical concept; common human reason,[a] indeed, agrees perfectly with this in its practical judgment, and has the principle just cited always before its eyes.

Let the question be, e.g.: When I am in a tight spot, may I not make a promise with the intention of not keeping it? Here I easily make a distinction in the signification the question can have, whether it is prudent, or whether it is in conformity with duty, to make a false promise. The first can without doubt often occur. I do see very well that it is not sufficient to get myself out of a present embarrassment by means of this subterfuge, but rather it must be reflected upon whether from this lie there could later arise much greater inconvenience than that from which I am now freeing myself, and, since the consequences of my supposed *cleverness* are not so easy to foresee, and a trust once lost to me might become much more disadvantageous than any ill I think I am avoiding, whether it might not be more *prudent* to conduct myself in accordance with a universal maxim and make it into a habit not to promise anything except with the intention of keeping it. Yet it soon occurs to me here that such a maxim has as its ground only the worrisome consequences. Now to be truthful from duty is something entirely different from being truthful out of worry over

---

and yet also as in itself necessary. As a law we are subject to it without asking permission of self-love; as laid upon us by ourselves, it is a consequence of our will, and has from the first point of view an analogy with fear, and from the second with inclination. All respect for a person is properly only respect for the law (of uprightness, etc.) of which the person gives us the example. Because we regard the expansion of our talents also as a duty, we represent to ourselves a person with talents also as an *example of a law,* as it were (to become similar to the person in this) and that constitutes our respect. [The bracketed clause in this sentence was added in 1786.] All so-called moral *interest* consists solely in *respect* for the law.[12]

a. 1785: "but common human reason . . ."

disadvantageous consequences; in the first case, the concept of the action in itself already contains a law for me, whereas in the second I must look around elsewhere to see which effects might be bound up with it for me. For if I deviate from the principle of duty, then this is quite certainly evil; but if I desert my maxim of prudence, then that can sometimes be very advantageous to me, even though it is safer to remain with it. Meanwhile, to inform myself in the shortest and least deceptive way in regard to my answer to this problem, whether a lying promise is in conformity with duty, I ask myself: would I be content with it if my maxim (of getting myself out of embarrassment through an untruthful promise) should be valid as a universal law (for myself as well as others), and would I be able to say to myself that anyone may make an untruthful promise when he finds himself in embarrassment which he cannot get out of in any other way? Then I soon become aware that I can will the lie but not at all a universal law to lie; for in accordance with such a law there would properly be no promises, because it would be pointless to avow my will in regard to my future actions to those who would not believe this avowal, or, if they rashly did so, who would pay me back in the same coin; hence my maxim, as soon as it were made into a universal law, would destroy itself.

Thus I need no well-informed shrewdness to know what I have to do in order to make my volition morally good. Inexperienced in regard to the course of the world, incapable of being prepared for all the occurrences that might eventuate in it, I ask myself only: Can you will also that your maxim should become a universal law? If not, then it is reprehensible, and this not for the sake of any disadvantage impending for you or someone else, but because it cannot fit as a principle into a possible universal legislation; but for this legislation reason compels immediate respect from me, from which, to be sure, I still do not have *insight* into that on which it is grounded (which the philosopher may investigate), but I at least understand this much, that it is an estimation of a worth which far outweighs everything whose worth is commended by inclination, and that the necessity of my actions from *pure* respect for the practical law is what constitutes duty, before which every other motive must give way because it is the condition of a will that is good *in itself,* whose worth surpasses everything.

Thus in the moral cognition of common human reason we have attained to its principle, which it obviously does not think abstractly in such a universal form, but actually has always before its eyes and uses as its standard of judgment. It would be easy here to show how, with this compass in its

[Ak 4:403]

[Ak 4:404]

hand, it knows its way around very well in all the cases that come before it, how to distinguish what is good, what is evil, what conforms to duty or is contrary to duty, if, without teaching it the least new thing, one only makes it aware of its own principle, as Socrates did;[13] and thus that it needs no science and philosophy to know what one has to do in order to be honest and good, or indeed, even wise and virtuous. It might even have been conjectured in advance that the acquaintance with what every human being is obliged to do, hence to know, would also be the affair of everyone, even of the most common human being. Here[a] one cannot regard without admiration the way the practical faculty of judgment is so far ahead of the theoretical in the common human understanding. In the latter, if common reason ventures to depart from the laws of experience and perceptions of sense, then it falls into sheer inconceivabilities and self-contradictions, or at least into a chaos of uncertainty, obscurity, and inconstancy. But in the practical, the power of judgment first begins to show itself to advantage when the common understanding excludes from practical laws all sensuous incentives. It then even becomes subtle, caviling with its conscience, or with other claims in reference to what is to be called right, or even in wanting sincerely to determine the worth of actions for its own instruction,[b] and, what is most striking, it can in the latter case do so with just as good a hope of getting things right as any philosopher might promise to do; indeed, it is almost more secure in this even than the latter, because the philosopher has[c] no other principle than the common understanding, but the philosopher's judgment is easily confused by a multiplicity of considerations that are alien and do not belong to the matter and can make it deviate from the straight direction. Would it not accordingly be more advisable in moral things to stay with the judgment of common reason, and bring in philosophy at most only in order to exhibit the system of morals all the more completely and comprehensibly, and its rules in a way that is more convenient for their use (still more for disputation), but not in order to remove the common human understanding in a practical respect out of its happy simplicity, and through philosophy to set it on a new route of investigation and instruction?

There is something splendid about innocence, but it is in turn a very bad thing that it cannot be protected very well and is easily seduced. On this   [Ak 4:405]

a. 1785: "Nevertheless"
b. 1785: *Belohnung* ('reward'); 1786: *Belehrung* ('instruction')
c. 1785: "can have"

account even wisdom—which consists more in conduct[a] than in knowledge—also needs science, not in order to learn from it but in order to provide entry and durability for its precepts. The human being feels in himself a powerful counterweight against all commands of duty, which reason represents to him as so worthy of esteem, in his needs and inclinations, whose satisfaction he summarizes under the name of 'happiness'. Now reason commands its precepts unremittingly, without promising anything to inclinations, thus snubbing and disrespecting, as it were, those impetuous claims, which at the same time seem so reasonable (and will not be done away with by any command). From this, however, arises a *natural dialectic,* that is, a propensity to ratiocinate against those strict laws of duty and to bring in doubt their validity, or at least their purity and strictness, and[b] where possible, to make them better suited to our wishes and inclinations, i.e. at ground to corrupt them and deprive them of their entire dignity, which not even common practical reason can in the end call good.

Thus *common human reason* is impelled, not through any need of speculation (which never assaults it as long as it is satisfied with being mere healthy reason), but rather from practical grounds themselves, to go outside its sphere and to stake a step into the field of *practical philosophy,* in order to receive information and distinct directions about the source of its principle and its correct determination in opposition to the maxims based on need and inclination, so that it may escape from its embarrassment concerning the claims of both sides and not run the risk of being deprived, through the ambiguity into which it easily falls, of all genuine ethical principles. Thus even in common practical reason, when it is cultivated, there ensues unnoticed a *dialectic,* which necessitates it to seek help in philosophy, just as befalls it in its theoretical use; and therefore the first will find no more tranquillity than the other anywhere except in a complete critique of our reason.

a. *Tun und Lassen*
b. 1785: "at least"

Second section

Transition from popular moral philosophy
to
the metaphysics of morals

If we have thus far drawn our concept of duty from the common use of our practical reason, it is by no means to be inferred from this that we have treated it as a concept of experience. Rather, if we attend to the experience of the conduct[a] of human beings, we encounter frequent and, as we ourselves concede, just complaints that one could cite no safe examples of the disposition to act from pure duty; that, even if some of what is done may *accord* with what *duty* commands, nevertheless it always[b] remains doubtful whether[c] it is really done *from duty* and thus has a moral worth. Hence[d] in all ages there have been philosophers who have absolutely denied the actuality of this disposition in human actions, and have ascribed everything to a more or less refined self-love, yet without bringing the correctness of the concept of morality into doubt; rather, with inward regret they have made mention[e] of the fragility and impurity of human nature,[1] which is, to be sure, noble enough to make an idea so worthy of respect into its precept, but at the same time is too weak to follow it, and uses reason, which ought to serve it for legislation, only in order to take care of the interest of inclinations, whether singly or at most in their greatest compatibility with one another.

In fact it is absolutely impossible to settle with complete certainty   through experience whether there is even a single case where the maxim of an otherwise dutiful action has rested solely on moral grounds and on the representation of one's duty. For it is sometimes the case that with the most acute self-examination we encounter nothing that could have been powerful enough apart from the moral ground of duty to move us to this or

---

a. *Tun und Lassen*

b. 1785: "thus" instead of "always"

c. 1785: "that" instead of "whether"

d. 1785 omits this word and treats this sentence as a subordinate clause connected to the previous sentence.

e. 1786 adds the verb construction *Erwähnung taten*, which was missing in 1785.

that good action and to so great a sacrifice; but from this it cannot be safely inferred that it was not actually some covert impulse of self-love, under the mere false pretense of that idea, that was the real determining cause of the will; so we would gladly flatter ourselves with a false presumption of a nobler motive, while in fact even through the most strenuous testing, we can never fully get behind the covert incentives, because when we are talking about moral worth, it does not depend on the actions, which one sees, but on the inner principles, which one does not see.[2]

One cannot better serve the wishes of those who ridicule all morality, as a mere figment of the mind overreaching itself through self-conceit, than to concede to them that the concepts of duty must be drawn solely from experience (as one is gladly persuaded, for the sake of convenience, in the case of all other concepts); for in this way one prepares for them a certain triumph. From love of humanity I will concede that most of our actions are in conformity with duty; but if one looks more closely at "the imagination of the thoughts of their hearts,"[a] then everywhere one runs into the dear self, which is always thrusting itself forward;[4] it is upon this that the aim is based, and not on the strict command of duty, which would often demand self-renunciation. One does not need to be an enemy of virtue, but only a cold-blooded observer, who does not take the liveliest wish for the good straightway as its reality, in order (especially with advancing years, and a power of judgment grown shrewder through experience and more acute for observation) to become doubtful at certain moments whether any true virtue is ever really to be encountered in the world. And here nothing can protect us from falling away entirely from our ideas of duty and preserve in our soul a well-grounded respect toward its law, except the clear conviction that even if there have never been actions that have arisen from such pure sources, yet nevertheless we are not talking here about whether this or that happens, but rather reason commands, for itself and independently of all appearances, what ought to happen; hence actions, of which perhaps the world has up to now given no example and about which one might, grounding everything on experience, very much doubt even their feasibility, are nevertheless commanded unremittingly by reason; and that e.g. pure honesty in friendship can no less be demanded of every human being, even if up to now there may not have been a single honest friend,[5] because this duty, as duty in general, lies prior to all experience in the idea of a reason determining the will through *a priori* grounds.

[Ak 4:408]

a. *ihr Dichten und Trachten*[3]

If one adds that unless one wants to dispute whether the concept of morality has any truth and relation to any possible object, one could not deny that its law is of such an extensive significance that it would have to be valid not merely for human beings but for all *rational beings in general,* and not merely under contingent conditions and with exceptions, but with *absolute necessity,* then it is clear that no experience could give occasion for inferring even the possibility of such apodictic laws.[6] For with what right could we bring into unlimited respect, as a universal precept for every rational nature, that which is perhaps valid only under the contingent conditions of humanity, and how should laws for the determination of *our* will be taken as laws for the determination of the will of a rational being in general, and only as such also for our will, if they were merely empirical and did not take their origin fully *a priori* from pure but practical reason?

Nor could one give worse advice to morality than by trying to get it from examples. For every example of morality that is to be represented to me as such must itself be previously judged in accordance with principles of morality as to whether it is worthy to serve as an original[a] example, i.e. as a model; but it can by no means by itself[b] supply the concept of morality. Even the holy one of the Gospel must first be compared with our ideal of moral perfection before one can recognize him as holy; he says this about himself too: Why do you call me (whom you see) good? No one is good (the archetype of the good) except the one God (whom you do not see).[7] But where do we get the concept of God as the highest good? Solely   [Ak 4:409] from the *idea* that reason projects *a priori* of moral perfection and connects inseparably with the concept of a free will. In morality there is no imitation, and examples serve only for encouragement, i.e. they place beyond doubt the feasibility of what the law commands, they make intuitive what the practical rule expresses universally; but they can never justify setting aside their true original,[c] which lies in reason, and directing ourselves in accordance with examples.

If, then, there is no genuine supreme principle of morality which does not have to rest on pure reason independent of all experience, then I believe it is not necessary even to ask whether it is good to expound these concepts in general (*in abstracto*), as they, together with the principles belonging to them, are fixed *a priori,* provided that this cognition is distinguished from common cognition and is to be called 'philosophical'. But in our age this

a. 1785: "genuine"
b. *zu oberst*
c. *Original*

might well be necessary. For if one were to collect votes on which is to be preferred, a pure rational cognition abstracted from everything empirical, hence a metaphysics of morals, or popular practical philosophy, then one would soon guess on which side the preponderance[a] will fall.[8]

This condescension to popular concepts[b] is to be sure very laudable when the elevation to principles of pure reason has already been achieved to full satisfaction, and that would mean first *grounding* the doctrine of morals on metaphysics, but procuring *entry* for it by means of popularity, once it stands firm. But it is quite absurd to want to humor popularity in the first investigation, upon which depends the correctness of principles. Not only can this procedure never lay claim to the extremely rare merit of a true *philosophical popularity*, since there is no art in being commonly understandable if one relinquishes all well-grounded insight; this produces only a disgusting mish-mash of patched-together observations and half-reasoned principles, in which superficial minds revel, because there is always something serviceable for everyday chitchat, but which insightful people disregard, feeling confused and dissatisfied without being able to help themselves; yet philosophers, who can very well see through the

[Ak 4:410]   illusion,[c] find little hearing when for certain occasions they decry this supposed popularity, in order, through acquiring determinate insight, finally to gain the right to be popular.

One need only look at the essays on morality adapted to this favored taste; then one will sometimes encounter the particular vocation of human nature (but occasionally also the idea of a rational nature in general), sometimes perfection, sometimes happiness, here moral feeling, there fear of God, some of this and some of that, all in a wondrous mixture, without its occurring to anyone to ask whether the principles of morality are to be sought anywhere in the knowledge of human nature (which we can obtain only through experience); and if not, if these principles are to be encountered in pure concepts of reason, fully *a priori*, free from everything empirical, and nowhere else even in the smallest part, then one may seize the initiative by entirely separating this investigation as pure practical philosophy, or (if one may use such a disreputable term) as metaphysics* of morals, bringing it for itself alone to its entire completeness, and defer-

a. 1785: "the truth"
b. *Volksbegriffen*
c. *Blendwerk*

[Ak 4:410]   *One can, if one wants, distinguish the 'pure' philosophy of morals (metaphysics) from the 'applied' (namely to human nature) (just as 'pure' mathematics and 'pure' logic are distinguished from 'applied'). By this terminology one is directly ring the expectations of the public, which demands popularity, until the completion of this undertaking.

But such a fully isolated metaphysics of morals, mixed with no anthropology, no theology, with no physics or hyperphysics, still less with occult qualities (which one might call 'hypophysical'), is not only an indispensable substrate of all theoretical cognition of duties which is securely determined, but it is at the same time also a desideratum of the highest importance for the actual fulfillment of its precepts. For the pure representation of duty and the moral law in general, mixed with no alien addition from empirical stimuli, has, by way of reason alone (which thereby for the first time becomes aware that it can for itself be practical) an influence on the human heart so much more powerful than all other incentives* that might be summoned from the [Ak 4:411] empirical field, that reason, in the consciousness of its dignity, despises the latter, and can gradually become their master; in place of this, a mixed doctrine of morals, composed from incentives of feelings and inclinations and simultaneously from concepts of reason, must make the mind waver between motivations that cannot be brought under any principle, and can lead us only very contingently to the good, but often also to the evil.

From what we have adduced it is clear that all moral concepts have their seat and origin fully *a priori* in reason, and this as much in the most common human reason as in that reason which is in highest measure speculative; that these concepts cannot be abstracted from any empirical, and therefore mere contingent, cognition; that their dignity lies precisely in this purity of their origin, so that^a they serve us as supreme practical principles;

---

reminded that moral principles are not grounded on the peculiarities of human nature, but must be subsistent *a priori* for themselves; but from them human practical rules must be derivable, as for every rational nature.

*I have a letter from the late excellent *Sulzer*, in which he asks me what the cause [Ak 4:411] might be that the doctrines of virtue, however convincing they may be to reason, yet accomplish so little. My answer, through being prepared so as to be complete, came too late. Yet it is nothing except that the teachers have not brought their concepts to purity, and because they were trying to do too much by scaring up motivations to be morally good from everywhere, in trying to strengthen their medicine they ruin it. For the most common observation shows that when one represents an upright action as it is carried out with a steadfast soul even under the greatest temptations of distress or of enticement, separate from every intention for any advantage in this or in another world, it leaves far behind and eclipses every similar action which is affected even in the slightest with an alien incentive; it elevates the soul and inspires the wish to be able also to act that way. Even moderately young children feel this impression, and one should never represent duty to them otherwise than this.[9]

a. This connecting word added in 1786

that whatever one adds to them of the empirical, one withdraws that much from their genuine influence and from the unlimited worth of actions; that it is not only of the greatest necessity for theoretical aims, when it is merely a matter of speculation, but it is also of the greatest practical importance, to demand that their concepts and laws should be taken from pure reason, to expound them pure and unmixed, indeed, to determine the range of this entire practical or pure rational cognition, i.e. the entire faculty of pure practical reason; but not as speculative philosophy permits, or indeed at times finds necessary, making the principles dependent on the particular nature of human reason, but rather, since moral laws are to be valid for every rational being in general, to derive them from the universal concept of a rational being in general; and in such a way all morality, which needs anthropology for its *application* to human beings, must first be expounded completely, independently of anthropology, as pure philosophy, i.e. as metaphysics (which it is possible to do in this species of entirely separate cognitions); but we must also be conscious that without being in possession of this, it would be futile, I will not say to determine precisely for speculative judgment what is moral about duty in everything that conforms to duty, but that it would even be impossible in a common and practical use, chiefly in moral instruction, to ground morality on its genuine principles and thereby to effect pure moral dispositions and implant them in people's minds for the highest good of the world.[a]

[Ak 4:412]

But now in order to progress by natural steps in this work not merely from the common moral judgment (which is here worthy of great respect) to the philosophical, as has already been done, but also from a popular philosophy, that goes no further than it can get through groping by means of examples, up to metaphysics (which is not any longer held back by anything empirical and, since it must cover the entire sum-total of rational cognition of this kind, goes as far as ideas, where even examples desert us), we must follow and distinctly exhibit the practical faculty of reason from its universal rules of determination up to where the concept of duty arises from it.

Every thing in nature works in accordance with laws. Only a rational being has the faculty to act *in accordance with the representation* of laws, i.e. in accordance with principles, or a *will*. Since for the derivation of actions from laws *reason* is required, the will is nothing other than practical reason. If reason determines the will without exception, then the actions of such a being, which are recognized as objectively necessary, are also

a. *Vom höchsten Weltbesten*

subjectively necessary, i.e. the will is a faculty of choosing *only that* which reason, independently of inclination, recognizes as practically necessary, i.e. as good. But if reason for itself alone does not sufficiently determine the will, if the will is still subject to subjective conditions (to certain incentives) which do not always agree with the objective conditions, in a word, if the [Ak 4:413] will is not *in itself* fully in accord with reason (as it actually is with human beings), then the actions which are objectively recognized as necessary are subjectively contingent, and the determination of such a will, in accord with objective laws, is *necessitation,* i.e. the relation of objective laws to a will which is not thoroughly good is represented as the determination of the will of a rational being through grounds of reason to which, however, this will in accordance with its nature is not necessarily obedient.

The representation of an objective principle, insofar as it is necessitating for a will, is called a 'command' (of reason) and the formula of the command is called an **imperative**.

All imperatives are expressed through an *ought* and thereby indicate the relation of an objective law of reason to a will which in its subjective constitution is not necessarily determined by that law (a necessitation). They say that it would be good to do or refrain from something, but they say it to a will that does not always do something just because it is represented to it as good to do. Practical *good,* however, is that which determines the will by means of representations of reason, hence not from subjective causes, but objectively, i.e. from grounds that are valid for every rational being as such. It is distinguished from the *agreeable,* as that which has influence on the will only by means of sensation from merely subjective causes, those which are valid only for the senses of this or that one, and not as a principle of reason, which is valid for everyone.*

---

* The dependence of the faculty of desire on sensations is called 'inclination', [Ak 4:413] and this always therefore proves a *need*. But the dependence of a contingently determinable will on principles of reason is called an *interest*. This occurs, therefore, only with a dependent will, which does not always of itself accord with reason; with the divine will one cannot think of any interest. But the human will too can *take an interest* without therefore *acting from interest*. The former signifies the *practical* interest in the action, the second the *pathological* interest in the object of the action. The first indicates only the dependence of the will on principles of reason in itself, the second dependence on those principles of reason on behalf of inclination, where, namely, reason furnishes only the practical rule as to how the need of inclination is to be supplied. In the first case the action interests me, in the second the object of the action (insofar as it is agreeable to me). In the First Section we have [Ak 4:414] seen that with an action from duty it is not the interest in an object that has to be looked to, but merely the action itself and its principle in reason (the law).

[Ak 4:414]   A perfectly good will would thus stand just as much under objective laws (of the good), but it would not be possible to represent it as *necessitated* by them to lawful actions, because of itself, in accordance with its subjective constitution, it can be determined only through the representation of the good. Hence for the *divine* will, and in general for a *holy* will, no imperatives are valid; the *ought* is out of place[a] here, because the *volition* is of itself already necessarily in harmony with the law. Hence imperatives are only formulas expressing the relation of objective laws of volition in general to the subjective imperfection of the will of this or that rational being, e.g. to the human being.

Now all *imperatives* command either *hypothetically* or *categorically*. The former represent the practical necessity of a possible action as a means to attain something else that one wills (or which it is possible that one might will). The categorical imperative would be that one which represented an action as objectively necessary for itself, without any reference to another end.

Because every practical law represents a possible action as good, and therefore as necessary for a subject practically determinable by reason, all imperatives are formulas of the determination of action, which is necessary in accordance with the principle of a will which is good in some way.[b] Now if the action were good merely as a means to *something else,* then the imperative is *hypothetical;* if it is represented as good *in itself,* hence necessary, as the principle of the will, in a will that in itself accords with reason, then it is *categorical.*

The imperative thus says which action possible through me would be good, and represents the practical rule in relation to a will[c] which does not directly do an action because it is good, in part because the subject does not always know that it is good, in part because if it did know this, its maxims could still be contrary to the objective principles of a practical reason.

The hypothetical imperative thus says only that the action is good for
[Ak 4:415]   some *possible* or *actual* aim. In the first case it is a **problematically**,[10] in the second an **assertorically** practical principle. The categorical imperative, which declares the action for itself as objectively necessary without reference to any aim, i.e. also without any other end, is valid as an **apodictically** practical principle.

One can think of that which is possible only through the powers of some rational being also as a possible aim of any will, and hence the principles of

a. *am unrechten Orte*
b. 1785: "for some aim"
c. 1785: "the will"

the action, insofar as it is represented as necessary in order to achieve any aim to be effected through it, are infinitely many. All sciences have some practical part, consisting of the problems whether^a any end is possible for us and of imperatives about how it can be attained. These can therefore in general be called imperatives of **skill**. Whether the end is rational and good is not the question here, but only what one has to do in order to achieve them. The precepts for the physician, how to make his patient healthy in a well-grounded way, and for the poisoner, how to kill him with certainty,^b are to this extent of equal worth, since each serves to effect its aim perfectly. Because in early youth one does not know what ends he will run up against in life, parents seek chiefly to have their children learn *many things,* and they concern themselves about *skill* in the use of means toward all kinds of *discretionary* ends, about none of which they can determine whether it will perhaps actually become an aim of his pupil in the future, but about any of which, however, it is *possible* that he might someday have it, and this concern is so great that they commonly neglect to educate and correct their judgment over the worth of the things that they may perhaps make their ends.

There is *one* end, however, that one can presuppose as actual for all rational beings (insofar as imperatives apply to them, namely as dependent beings) and thus one aim that they not merely *can* have, but of which one can safely presuppose that without exception^c they *do have* it in accordance with a natural necessity, and that is the aim at *happiness.* The hypothetical imperative that represents the practical necessity of the action as a means to furthering happiness, is **assertoric.** One may expound it not merely as necessary to an uncertain, merely possible aim, but to an aim that one can presuppose safely and *a priori*^d with every human being, because it belongs to his essence.^e Now one can call skill in the choice of means to his own greatest well-being *prudence** in the narrowest sense. Thus the imperative [Ak 4:416]

a. *Aufgaben, daß . . . ,* a construction somewhat opaque in its meaning and al-most as awkward in German as "problems that" would be in English
b. *sicher,* which could also be translated 'safely'
c. *insgesamt*
d. "and a priori" added in 1786
e. 1785: "to his nature"
*The word 'prudence' is taken in a twofold sense; first it can bear the name of [Ak 4:416] 'worldly prudence' and in the second that of 'private prudence'. The first is the skill of a human being to have influence on others, in order to use them for his aims. The second is the insight to unite all these aims to his own enduring advantage. The lat-ter is really that to which the worth of the first is reduced, and about someone who is prudent in the first way but not in the second way one can better say that he is clever and sly, but on the whole imprudent.

that refers to the choice of means to one's own happiness, i.e. the precept of prudence, is always *hypothetical;* the action is commanded not absolutely but only a means to another aim.

Finally, there is one imperative which, without being grounded on any other aim to be achieved through a certain course of conduct as its condition, commands this conduct immediately. This imperative is **categorical**. It has to do not with the matter of the action and what is to result from it, but with the form and the principle from which it results; and what is essentially good about it consists in the disposition, whatever the result may be. This imperative may be called that **of morality**.

The volition in accordance with these three kinds of principles is also clearly distinguished by a *difference*ᵃ in the necessitation of the will. Now in order to make this noticeable too, I believe that the most suitable terminology to use in ordering them is to say that they are either *rules* of skill, or *counsels* of prudence, or *commands (laws)* of morality. For only *law* carries with it the concept of an *unconditional* and objective, hence universally valid *necessity,* and commands are laws that must be obeyed, i.e. followed even against inclination. The *giving of counsel* contains necessity, to be sure, but can be valid merely under a subjective, pleasingᵇ condition, whether this or that human being counts this or that toward his happiness; the categorical imperative, by contrast, is not limited by any condition, and as absolutely, although practically necessary, can be called quite authentically a command. One could also call the first imperative *technical* (belonging to art), the second *pragmatic** (to welfare), the third *moral* (belonging to free conduct in general, i.e. to morals).

[Ak 4:417]

Now the question arises: How are all these imperatives possible? This question does not demand the knowledge how to think the execution of the action that the imperative commands, but rather merely how to think the necessitation of the will that the imperative expresses in the problem. How an imperative of skill is to be possible probably needs no particular discussion. Whoever wills the end, also wills (insofar as reason has deci-

---

a. *Ungleichheit*, which might also be translated 'inequality'[11]

b. *gefälliger*; editors often emend this to *zufälliger*, 'contingent'

[Ak 4:417]

*It seems to me that the authentic signification of the word 'pragmatic' could be determined most precisely in this way. For those *sanctions* are called 'pragmatic' which really flow not from the rights of states, as necessary laws, but from *provision* for the general welfare. A *history* is written 'pragmatically' when it makes us *prudent*, i.e., teaches how the world could take care of its advantage better than, or at any rate at least as well as, the world of antiquity has done.

sive influence on his actions) the means that are indispensably necessary to it that are in his control. As far as volition is concerned, this proposition is analytic; for in the volition of an object, as my effect, is already thought my causality as an acting cause, i.e. the use of means; and the imperative extracts the concept of actions necessary for this end out of the concept of a volition of this end (to be sure, synthetic propositions belong to determining the means themselves to a proposed aim, but they have nothing to do with the ground, with making the act^a of the will actual, but rather with how to make the object actual). That in order to divide a line into two equal parts in accordance with a secure principle I must draw two arcs from its endpoints—this mathematics obviously teaches only through synthetic propositions; but that if I know that the specified effect can occur only through such an action, then if I completely will the effect, I would also will the action that is required for it—that is an analytic proposition; for to represent something as an effect possible through me in a certain way and to represent myself, in regard to it, acting in this same way—those are entirely the same.

Imperatives of prudence would be equally analytic, and entirely coincide with those of skill, if only it were so easy to provide a determinate concept of happiness. For here, as there, it would be said: whoever wills the end, also wills (necessarily in accord with reason) the sole means to it in his control. Yet it is a misfortune that the concept of happiness is such [Ak 4:418] an indeterminate concept that although every human being wishes to attain it, he can never say, determinately and in a way that is harmonious with himself, what he really wishes and wills. The cause of this is that all the elements that belong to the concept of happiness are altogether empirical, i.e. have to be gotten from experience, while for the idea of happiness an absolute whole, a maximum of welfare is required, in my present and in every future condition. Now it is impossible for the most insightful, and at the same time most resourceful, yet finite being to make a determinate concept of what he really wills here. If he wills wealth, how much worry, envy and harassment^b will he not bring down on his shoulders?^{c} If he wills much cognition and insight, perhaps that could only give him a more acute eye, to show him all the more terribly those ills that are now hidden from him and yet cannot be avoided, or to burden his desires, which already give him

a. *Aktus*
b. *Nachstellung*
c. Kant ends this sentence, which seems halfway between an assertion (or even an exclamation) and a rhetorical question, with a period rather than a question mark.

quite enough to do, with still more needs. If he wills a long life, who will guarantee him that it would not be a long misery? If he wills at least health, how often have bodily discomforts not deterred him from excesses into which unlimited health would have allowed him to fall, etc.? In short, he is not capable of determining with complete certainty, in accordance with any principle, what will make him truly happy, because omniscience would be required for that. Thus one cannot act in accordance with determinate principles in order to be happy, but only in accordance with empirical counsels, e.g. of diet, frugality, politeness, restraint, etc., of which experience teaches that they most promote welfare on the average. It follows from this that the imperatives of prudence, to speak precisely, cannot command at all, i.e. cannot exhibit actions objectively as practically *necessary;* that they are sooner to be taken as advisings (*consilia*) than as commands (*praecepta*) of reason; that the problem of determining, certainly[a] and universally, what action will promote the happiness of a rational being, is fully insoluble, hence no imperative in regard to it is possible, which would command us, in the strict sense, to do what would make us happy, because happiness is not an ideal of reason but of imagination, resting merely on empirical grounds, of which it would be futile to expect that they should determine an action through which to attain the totality of a series of consequences which are in fact infinite. This imperative of prudence, meanwhile, would be an analytically practical proposition if one assumes that the means to happiness could be specified with certainty;[b] for it is distinguished from the imperative of skill only in this, that with the latter the end is merely possible, but with the former it is given: since, however, both merely command the means to that which it is presupposed that one wills as an end, then the imperative that commands the volition of the means for him who wills the end is in both cases analytic. Thus there is also no difficulty in regard to the possibility of such an imperative.

[Ak 4:419]

By contrast, how the imperative of *morality* is possible, is without doubt the sole question in need of a solution, since it is not at all hypothetical and thus the necessity, represented as objective, cannot be based on any presupposition, as with the hypothetical imperatives. Yet in this connection it must not be left out of account that whether there is any such imperative anywhere cannot be settled *by any example,* hence not empirically; but the worry is rather that all those that seem categorical might be, in some hidden wise, hypothetical. E.g., if it is said: "You ought not to make a deceiving prom-

a. *sicher*
b. *sicher*

ise," and one assumes that the necessity of this omission is not mere advice for the avoidance of some ill or other, so that it might really mean: "You should not make a lying promise, so that if it were revealed then you would lose your credit"; if an action of this kind[a] must be considered as evil for itself, then the imperative forbidding it would be categorical; then one still cannot with certainty give an example where the will is determined merely by the law, without any other incentive, although it might[b] appear so; for it is always possible that fear of disgrace, or perhaps also an obscure worry about other dangers, might secretly have had an influence on the will. Who[c] can prove through experience the nonexistence of a cause, since experience teaches us nothing beyond the fact that we do not perceive one? But in such a case the so-called moral imperative, that appears as such to be categorical and unconditioned, would in fact be only a pragmatic precept, which alerts us to our own advantage and merely teaches us to pay attention to it.

Thus we will have to investigate the possibility of a *categorical* imperative entirely *a priori,* since here we cannot have the advantage that its reality is given in experience, so that its possibility would be necessary not for its establishment but only for its explanation.[d] Meanwhile,[e] we can provisionally have insight into this much: that the categorical imperative alone can be stated as a practical **law**, while the others collectively are, to be sure, *principles* of the will, but cannot be called 'laws'; for what it is necessary to do for the attainment of a discretionary aim can be considered in itself to be contingent, and we can always be rid of the precept if we give up the aim; whereas the unconditioned command leaves the will no free discretion in regard to the opposite, hence it alone carries with it that necessity which we demand for a law.

Secondly, with this categorical imperative, or law of morality, the ground of difficulty (of having insight into its possibility) is very great indeed. It is a synthetically practical proposition* *a priori,* and since there

[Ak 4:420]

a. 1785: "but rather if one asserts that an action of this kind . . ."
b. 1785: "even if it might appear so"
c. 1785: "For who . . ."
d. *Erklärung,* which could also be translated 'definition'[12]
e. 1785: "But we can provisionally . . ."
*I connect the deed *a priori* with the will, without a presupposed condition from any inclination, hence necessarily (although only objectively, i.e. under the idea of reason, which would have full control over all subjective motivations). This is therefore a practical proposition that does not derive the volition of an action analytically from any other volition already presupposed (for we have no such perfect will), but is immediately connected with the concept of the will of a rational being, as something not contained in it.

[Ak 4:420]

is so much difficulty in gaining insight into the possibility of propositions of this kind in theoretical cognition, it is easy to gather that there will be no less in the practical.

Regarding this problem we will first try to see whether perhaps the mere concept of a categorical imperative does not also provide us with its formula, containing the proposition which alone can be a categorical imperative; for how such an absolute command is possible, even if we know how it is stated, will still demand particular and difficult effort, which, however, we will postpone until the last section.

If I think of a *hypothetical* imperative in general, then I do not know beforehand what it will contain until the condition is given to me. But if I think of a *categorical* imperative, then I know directly what it contains. For since besides the law, the imperative contains only the necessity of the [Ak 4:421]   maxim,* that it should accord with this law, but the law contains no condition to which it is limited, there remains nothing left over with which the maxim of the action is to be in accord, and this accordance alone is what the imperative really represents necessarily.

The categorical imperative is thus only a single one, and specifically this: *Act only in accordance with that maxim through which you at the same time can will that it become a universal law.*

Now if from this one imperative all imperatives of duty can be derived as from their principle, then although we leave unsettled whether in general what one calls 'duty' is an empty concept, we can at least indicate what we are thinking in the concept of duty and what this concept means.ᵃ

Because the universality of the law in accordance with which effects happen constitutes that which is really called *nature* in the most general sense (in accordance with its form), i.e. the existence of things insofar as it is determined in accordance with universal laws, thus the universal imperative of duty can also be stated as follows: *So act, as if the maxim of your action were to become through your will a* **universal law of nature**.

[Ak 4:420]   *A *maxim* is the subjective principle for action, and must be distinguished from the *objective principle,* namely the practical law. The former contains the practical [Ak 4:421]   rule that reason determines in accord with the conditions of the subject (often its ignorance or also its inclinations), and is thus the principle in accordance with which the subject *acts;* but the law is the objective principle, valid for every rational being, and the principle in accordance with which it *ought to act,* i.e. an imperative.

   a. *sagen wolle*

Now we will enumerate[a] some duties, in accordance with their usual division into duties toward ourselves and toward other human beings, and into perfect and imperfect duties:*

1) One person, through a series of ills[b] that have accumulated to the point of hopelessness, feels weary of life but is still so far in possession of [Ak 4:422] his reason that he can ask himself whether it might be contrary to the duty to himself to take his own life. Now he tries out whether the maxim of his action could become a universal law of nature. But his maxim is: "From self-love, I make it my principle to shorten my life when by longer term it threatens more ill than it promises agreeableness." The question is whether this principle of self-love could become a universal law of nature. But then one soon sees that a nature whose law it was to destroy life through the same feeling[c] whose vocation it is to impel the furtherance of life would contradict itself, and thus could not subsist as nature; hence that maxim could not possibly obtain as a universal law of nature, and consequently it entirely contradicts the supreme principle of all duty.

2) Another sees himself pressured by distress[d] into borrowing money. He knows very well that he will not be able to pay, but he also sees that nothing will be lent him if he does not firmly promise to pay at a determinate time. He wants to make such a promise; yet he has conscience enough to ask himself: "Is it not impermissible and contrary to duty to get out of distress in such a way?" Supposing he nevertheless resolved on it, his maxim would be stated as follows: "If I believe myself to be in a financial emergency,[e] then I will borrow money and promise to pay it back, although I know this will never happen." Now this principle of self-love, or of what is expedient for oneself, might perhaps be united with my entire future welfare, yet the question now is: "Is it right?" I thus transform this

---

a. *herzählen*, which could also be translated as 'reckon' or 'calculate'

*Here one must note well that I reserve the division of duties entirely for a future [Ak 4:421] *metaphysics of morals;* the division here therefore stands only as a discretionary one (to order my examples). For the rest, I understand by a perfect duty that which permits no exception to the advantage of inclination, and I do have *perfect duties* that are not merely external but also internal, which runs contrary to the use of words common in the schools; but I do not mean to defend that here, because for my aim it is all the same whether or not one concedes it to me.[13]

b. *Übeln*

c. *Empfindung*

d. *Not,* which could also be translated 'necessity' or 'emergency'

e. *Geldnot*[14]

claim[a] of self-love into a universal law and set up the question thus: "How would it stand if my maxim became a universal law?" Yet I see right away that it could never be valid as a universal law of nature and still agree with itself, but rather it would necessarily contradict itself. For the universality of a law that everyone who believes himself to be in distress could promise whatever occurred to him with the intention of not keeping it would make impossible the promise and the end one might have in making it, since no one would believe that anything has been promised him, but rather would deride every such utterance as vain pretense.

3) A third finds in himself a talent, which could, by means of some cultivation, make him into a human being who is useful for all sorts of aims. But he sees himself as in comfortable circumstances and sooner prefers[b] to indulge in gratification than to trouble himself with the expansion and improvement of his fortunate natural predispositions. Yet he still asks whether, apart from the agreement of his maxim of neglecting his gifts of nature with his propensity to amusement, it also agrees with what one calls 'duty'. Then he sees that, although a nature could still subsist in accordance with such a universal law, though then the human being (like the South Sea Islanders) would think only of letting his talents rust and applying his life merely to idleness, amusement, procreation, in a word, to enjoyment; yet it is impossible for him to **will** that this should become a universal law of nature, or that it should be implanted in us as such by natural instinct. For as a rational being he necessarily wills that all the faculties in him should be developed, because they are serviceable and given to him for[c] all kinds of possible aims.

4)[d] Yet a *fourth*—for whom it is going well, while he sees that others have to struggle with great hardships (with which he could well help them)—thinks: "What has it to do with me? Let each be as happy as heaven wills, or as he can make himself, I will not take anything from him or even envy him; only I do not want to contribute to his welfare or to his assistance in distress!"[e] Now to be sure, if such a way of thinking were to become a universal law of nature, then the human race could well subsist, and without doubt still better than when everyone chatters about sympa-

a. *Zumutung*

b. 1785: "and he prefers it that he indulge . . ."

c. "and given" added in 1786

d. Kant's text, though it emphasizes the word 'fourth', omits the '4)' required by the parallel with his three other examples.

e. *Not*

thetic participation[a] and benevolence, and even on occasion exerts himself to practice them, but, on the contrary also deceives wherever he[b] can, sells out or otherwise infringes on the right of human beings. But although it is possible that a universal law of nature could well subsist in accordance with that maxim, yet it is impossible to **will** that such a principle should be valid without exception[c] as a natural law. For a will that resolved on this would conflict with itself, since the case could sometimes arise in which he needs the love and sympathetic participation of others, and where, through such a natural law arising from his own will, he would rob himself of all the hope of assistance that he wishes for himself.

Now these are some of the many actual duties, or at least of what we take to be duties, whose partitioning[d] from the single principle just adduced clearly meets the eye. One must *be able to will* that a maxim of our action should become a universal law: this is the canon of the moral judgment of this action in general. Some actions are so constituted that their maxim cannot even be *thought* without contradiction as a universal law of nature, much less could one *will* that it *ought* to become one. With others, that internal impossibility is not to be encountered, but it is impossible to *will* that their maxims should be elevated to the universality of a natural law, because such a will would contradict itself. One easily sees that the first conflict with strict or narrow (unremitting) duty, the second only with wide (meritorious) duty, and thus all duties, regarding the kind of obligation (not the object of their action) have been completely set forth[e] through these examples in their dependence on the one principle.   [Ak 4:424]

Now if we attend to ourselves in every transgression of a duty, then we find that we do not actually will that our maxim should become a universal law, for that is impossible for us, but rather will that its opposite should remain a law generally; yet we take the liberty of making an *exception* for ourselves, or (even only for this once) for the advantage of our inclination. Consequently, if we weighed everything from one and the same point of view, namely that of reason, then we would encounter a contradiction in our own will, namely that objectively a certain principle should be necessary as a universal law and yet subjectively that it should not be universally valid,

a. *Teilnehmung*
b. 1785: "wherever one can"
c. *allenthalben*
d. *Abteilung*[15]
e. 1785: "are completely set forth . . ."

but rather that it should admit of exceptions. But since we consider our action at one time from a point of view that accords entirely with reason, and then, however, also the same action from the point of view of a will affected by inclination, there is actually no contradiction here, but only a resistance of inclination against the precept of reason (*antagonismus*), through which the universality of the principle (*universalitas*) is transformed into a mere general validity (*generalitas*), so that the practical principle of reason is supposed to meet the maxim halfway. Now although this cannot be justified in our own impartially rendered judgment, it proves that we actually recognize the validity of the categorical imperative and (with every respect for it) allow ourselves only a few exceptions, which are, as it seems to us, insignificant and forced upon us.

[Ak 4:425]   Thus we have established at least this much: that if duty is a concept that is to contain significance and actual legislation for our actions, then this duty could be expressed only in categorical imperatives, but by no means in hypothetical ones; likewise, which is already quite a bit, we have exhibited distinctly and for every use the content of the categorical imperative which would have to contain the principle of all duty (if there is such a thing at all). But we are still not ready to prove *a priori* that there actually is such an imperative, that there is a practical law which commands for itself absolutely and without any incentives, and that it is a duty to follow this law.

With the aim of attaining that, it is of the utmost importance to let this serve as a warning that one must not let it enter his mind to try to derive the reality of this principle from the *particular quality of human nature*. For duty ought to be the practically unconditioned necessity of action; thus it must be valid for all rational beings (for only to them can an imperative apply at all), and must *only for this reason* be a law for every human will. That which, by contrast, is derived only from what is proper to the particular natural predisposition of humanity, or from certain feelings and propensities, or indeed, if possible, from a particular direction of human reason, and would not have to be valid necessarily for the will of every rational being — that can, to be sure, be a maxim for us, but cannot yield any law; it can yield a subjective principle, in accordance with which we may have a propensity and inclination, but not an objective one, in accordance with which we would be *assigned* to act, even if it were to go directly contrary to all our propensities, inclinations, and natural adaptations; it even proves all the more the sublimity and inner dignity of the command in a duty, the less subjective causes are for it and the more they are against it, without on this account the least weakening the necessitation through the law or taking anything away from its validity.

Now here we see philosophy placed in fact at a perilous standpoint, which is to be made firm, regardless of anything either in heaven or on earth from which it may depend or by which it may be supported. Here it should prove its purity[a] as self-sustainer of its own laws, not as a herald of those that an implanted sense or who knows what tutelary nature whispers to it, which, taken collectively, though they may be better than nothing at all, yet they can never yield the principles that reason dictates and which must have their source fully *a priori* and therewith at the same time their commanding authority: expecting nothing of the inclination of the human being, but everything from the supremacy of the law and the respect owed to it; or else, if that fails, condemning the human being to self-contempt and inner abhorrence. [Ak 4:426]

Thus everything that is empirical is, as a contribution toward the principle of morality, not only entirely unfit for it, but even highly disadvantageous to the purity[b] of morals themselves, in which precisely consists the sublime[16] worth of a will absolutely good in itself and elevated above all price,[17] that the principle of the actions is free of all influences of contingent grounds that only experience can provide. One cannot be given too many or too frequent warnings against this negligent or even base way of thinking, that seeks out the principle among empirical motivations and laws, since human reason in its weariness gladly reposes on this pillow and, in the dream of sweet illusions[c] (which lets it embrace a cloud instead of Juno),[18] supplants the place of morality with a bastard patched together from limbs of quite diverse ancestry, which looks similar to whatever anyone wants to see, but not to virtue, for him who has once beheld it in its true shape.*

The question is therefore this: Is it a necessary law *for all rational beings* to judge their actions always in accordance with those maxims of which they themselves can will that they should serve as universal laws? If it is, then it must be bound up (fully *a priori*) with the concept of the will of a rational being in general. But in order to discover this connection, one must, however much one may resist it, take one step beyond, namely to

a. *Lauterkeit*
b. *Lauterkeit*
c. *Vorspiegelungen*
*To behold virtue in its authentic shape is nothing other than to exhibit morality [Ak 4:426] denuded of all admixture of the sensible and all ungenuine adornment of reward or self-love. How completely it eclipses everything else that appears charming to inclinations, everyone can easily be aware of by means of the least attempt of his reason, if it is not entirely corrupted for abstraction.

metaphysics, although into a domain of metaphysics that is distinguished from that of speculative philosophy, namely into the metaphysics of morals.

In a practical philosophy, where what is to be established are not grounds for what *happens,* but laws for what *ought to happen,* even if it never does happen, i.e. objectively practical laws, there we do not find it necessary to institute an investigation into the grounds why something pleases or displeases, how the gratification of mere sensation is to be distinguished from taste, and whether the latter is distinct from a universal satisfaction of reason; on what the feelings of pleasure and displeasure rest, and how from them arise desires and inclinations, and from these, again, through the co-operation of reason, maxims arise; for that all belongs to an empirical doctrine of the soul, which constitutes the second part of the doctrine of nature, if one considers it as *philosophy of nature* insofar as it is grounded on *empirical laws.* Here, however, we are talking about objectively practical laws, hence about the relation of a will to itself insofar as it determines itself merely through reason, such that everything that has reference to the empirical falls away of itself; because if *reason for itself alone* determines conduct (the possibility of which we will investigate right now), it must necessarily do this *a priori.*

The will is thought as a faculty of determining itself to action *in accord with the representation of certain laws.* And such a faculty can be there to be encountered only in rational beings. Now that which serves the will as the objective ground of its self-determination is the *end,* and this, if it is given through mere reason, must be equally valid for all rational beings. By contrast, what contains merely the ground of the possibility of the action whose effect is the end is called the *means.* The subjective ground of desire is the *incentive,* the objective ground of volition is the *motive;* hence the distinction between subjective ends, that rest on incentives, and objective ones, that depend on motives which are valid for every rational being. Practical principles are *formal* when they abstract from all subjective ends; but they are *material* when they are grounded on these, hence on certain incentives. The ends that a rational being proposes as *effects* of its action at its discretion (material ends) are all only relative; for only their relation to a particular kind of faculty of desire of the subject gives them their worth, which therefore can provide no necessary principles valid universally for all rational beings and hence valid for every volition, i.e. practical laws. Hence all these relative ends are only the ground of hypothetical imperatives.

But suppose there were something *whose existence in itself* had an absolute worth, something that, as *end in itself,* could be a ground of determinate laws; then in it and only in it alone would lie the ground of a possible categorical imperative, i.e. of a practical law.

Now I say that the human being and in general every rational being *exists* as end in itself, *not merely as means* to the discretionary use of this or that will, but in all its actions, those directed toward itself as well as those directed toward other rational beings, it must always *at the same time* be considered as an *end*. All objects of inclinations have only a conditioned worth; for if the inclinations and the needs grounded on them did not exist, then their object would be without worth. The inclinations themselves, however, as sources of needs, are so little of absolute worth, to be wished for in themselves, that rather to be entirely free of them must be the universal wish of every rational being.[19] Thus the worth of all objects *to be acquired* through our action is always conditioned. The beings whose existence rests not on our will but on nature, nevertheless have, if they are beings without reason, only a relative worth as means, and are called *things;* rational beings, by contrast, are called *persons,* because their nature already marks them out as ends in themselves, i.e. as something that may not be used merely as means, hence to that extent limits all arbitrary choice[a] (and is an object of respect). These are not merely subjective ends whose existence as effect of our action has a worth *for us;* but rather *objective ends,* i.e. things whose existence in itself is an end, and specifically an end such that no other end can be set in place of it, to which it should do service *merely* as means, because without this nothing at all of *absolute worth* would be encountered anywhere; but if all worth were conditioned, hence contingent, then for reason no supreme practical principle could anywhere be encountered.

If, then, there is supposed to be a supreme practical principle, and in regard to the human will a categorical imperative, then it must be such from the representation of that which, being necessarily an end for everyone, because it is an *end in itself,* constitutes an *objective* principle of the will, [Ak 4:429] hence can serve as a universal practical law. The ground of this principle is: *Rational nature exists as end in itself.* The human being necessarily represents his own existence in this way;[20] thus to that extent it is a *subjective* principle of human actions. But every other rational being also represents his existence in this way as consequent on the same rational ground as is valid for me;* thus it is at the same time an *objective* principle, from which, as a supreme practical ground, all laws of the will must be able to

a. *Willkür*

*This proposition I here set forth as a postulate. In the last section one will find   [Ak 4:429]
the grounds for it.[21]

be derived. The practical imperative will thus be the following: *Act so that you use humanity,*[22] *as much in your own person as in the person of every other, always at the same time as end and never merely as means.* We will see whether this can be accomplished.

In order to remain with the previous examples,

First, in accordance with the concept of the necessary duty toward one-self, the one who has suicide in mind will ask himself whether his action could subsist together with the idea of humanity *as an end in itself.* If he destroys himself in order to flee from a burdensome condition, then he makes use of a person merely as *a means,* for the preservation of a bearable condition up to the end of life. The human being, however, is not a thing, hence not something that can be used *merely* as a means, but must in all his actions always be considered as an end in itself. Thus I cannot dispose of the human being in my own person, so as to maim, corrupt, or kill him.[23] (The nearer determination of this principle, so as to avoid all misunderstanding, e.g. the amputation of limbs in order to preserve myself, or the risk at which I put my life in order to preserve my life, etc., I must here pass over; they belong to morals proper.)[a,24]

Second, as to the necessary or owed duty toward others, the one who has it in mind to make a lying promise to another will see[b] right away that he wills to make use of another human being *merely as means,* without the end also being contained in this other. For the one I want to use for my aims through such a promise cannot possibly be in harmony with my way of [Ak 4:430] conducting myself toward him and thus contain in himself the end of this action.[25] Even more distinctly does this conflict with the principle of other human beings meet the eye if one approaches it through examples of attacks on the freedom and property of others. For then it is clearly evident that the one who transgresses the rights of human beings is disposed to make use of the person of others merely as a means, without taking into consideration that as rational beings, these persons ought always to be esteemed at the same time as ends, i.e. only as beings who have to be able to contain in themselves the end of precisely the same action.*

---

a. *zur eigentlichen Moral*
b. *einsehen*

[Ak 4:430]   *Let one not think that the trivial *quod tibi non vis fieri, etc.* [What you do not want to be done to yourself do not do to another] could serve here as a standard or principle. For it is only derived from that principle, although with various limitations; it cannot be a universal law, for it does not contain the ground of duties toward oneself, nor that of the duties of love toward others (for many would gladly acquiesce that others should not be beneficent to him, if only he might be

Third, in regard to the contingent (meritorious) duty toward oneself, it is not enough that the action does not conflict with humanity in our person as end in itself, it must also *harmonize with it.* Now in humanity there are predispositions to greater perfection, which belong to ends of nature in regard to the humanity in our subject; to neglect these would at most be able to subsist with the *preservation* of humanity as end in itself, but not with the *furthering* of this end.

Fourth, as to the meritorious duty toward others, the natural end that all human beings have is their own happiness. Now humanity would be able to subsist if no one contributed to the happiness of others, yet did not intentionally remove anything from it; only this is only a negative and not a positive agreement with *humanity as end in itself,* if everyone does not aspire, as much as he can, to further the ends of others. For regarding the subject which is an end in itself: if that representation is to have its *total* effect on me, then its ends must as far as possible also be *my* ends.

This principle of humanity and of every rational nature in general *as end in itself* (which is the supreme limiting condition of the freedom of the ac- [Ak 4:431] tions of every human being), is not gotten from experience, first on account of its universality, since it applies to all rational beings in general, and no experience is sufficient to determine anything about that; second, because in it humanity is represented not as an end of human beings[a] (subjectively), i.e. as an object that one actually from oneself makes into an end, but as an objective end which, whatever ends we may have, is to constitute as a law the supreme limiting condition of all subjective ends, hence must arise from pure reason. The ground of all practical legislation, namely, lies *objectively in the rule* and the form of universality, which makes it capable of being a law (at least a law of nature) (in accordance with the first principle), but *subjectively* it lies in the *end;* but the subject of all ends is every rational being as end in itself (in accordance with the second principle): from this now follows the third practical principle of the will, as the supreme condition of its harmony with universal practical reason, the idea *of the will of every rational being as a will giving universal law.*

All maxims are repudiated in accordance with this principle which cannot subsist together with the will's own universal legislation. The will is thus not solely subject to the law,[b] but is subject in such a way that it must

---

relieved from showing beneficence to them), or finally of owed duties to one another, for the criminal would argue on this ground against the judge who punishes him, etc.[26]

a. 1785: "of the human being"
b. 1785: "not subject to the law except in such a way that . . ."

be regarded also *as legislating to itself,*[a] and precisely for this reason as subject to the law (of which it can consider itself as the author).[27]

Imperatives represented in the above way, namely of the lawfulness of actions generally similar to an *order of nature,* or of the universal *preference of the end* of rational beings themselves, just by being represented as categorical, excluded from their commanding authority all admixture of any interest as an incentive; but they were only *assumed* as categorical, because one had to assume such a thing if one wanted to explain the concept of duty. But that there are practical propositions which command categorically cannot be proven for itself here, just as little as this can still[b] happen anywhere in this section; yet one thing could have happened, namely that the withdrawal of all interest in the case of volition from duty, in the imperative itself, through any determination that it could contain, is indicated as the specific sign distinguishing the categorical from the hypothetical imperative, and this happens in the third formula of the principle, namely the idea of the will of every rational being as *a universally legislative will.*

[Ak 4:432]

For if we think of such a will, then although a will *that stands under laws* may be bound by means of an interest in this law, nevertheless it is impossible for a will that is itself supremely legislative to depend on any interest; for such a dependent will would need yet another law, that limited the interest of its self-love to the condition of a validity for the universal law.

Thus the *principle* of every human will as *a will legislating universally through all its maxims,** if otherwise everything were correct about it, would be quite *well suited* for the categorical imperative by the fact that precisely for the sake of the idea of universal legislation, it *grounds itself on no interest* and hence it alone among all[c] possible imperatives can be *unconditioned;* or still better, by converting the proposition, if there is a categorical imperative (i.e. a law for every will of a rational being), then it can command only that everything be done from the maxim of its will as a will that could at the same time have as its object itself as universally legislative; for only then is the practical principle and the imperative it obeys unconditioned, because it cannot have any interest at all as its ground.

a. 1785: "as a self-legislating [being]"
b. 1785: "just as little as this still cannot happen . . ."

[Ak 4:432]   *I can be exempted here from providing examples to elucidate this principle, since those that first elucidated the categorical imperative and its formula can all serve here for precisely that end.

c. This word added in 1786

Now it is no wonder, when we look back on all the previous efforts that have ever been undertaken to bring to light the principle of morality, why they all had to fail. One saw the human being bound through his duty to laws, but it did not occur to one that he was subject *only to his own* and yet *universal legislation,* and that he was obligated only to act in accord with his own will, which, however, in accordance with its natural end, is a universally legislative will. For if one thought of him only as subject to a law (whatever it might be), then this would have to bring with it some interest as a stimulus or coercion, because as a law it did not arise from *his* will, but rather this will was necessitated by *something else* to act in a certain way in conformity with the law. Through this entirely necessary consequence, however, all the labor of finding a supreme ground of duty was irretrievably lost. For from it one never got duty, but only necessity of action from a certain interest. Now this might be one's own interest or someone else's. But then the imperative always had to come out as conditioned, and could never work at all as a moral command. Thus I will call this principle[a] the principle of the *autonomy* of the will, in contrast to every[b] other, which on this account I count as *heteronomy.* [Ak 4:433]

The concept of every rational being that must consider itself as giving universal law through all the maxims of its will in order to judge itself and its actions from this point of view, leads to a very fruitful concept depending on it, namely that of *a realm of ends.*

By a *realm,* however, I understand the systematic combination of various rational beings through communal laws. Now because laws determine ends in accordance with their universal validity, there comes to be, if one abstracts from the personal differences between rational beings, as likewise from every content of their private ends, a whole of all ends — (of rational beings as ends in themselves, as well as of their own ends, which each may set for himself) in systematic connection, i.e. a realm of ends — can be thought, which is possible in accordance with the above principles.

For rational beings all stand under the *law* that every one of them ought to[c] treat itself and all others *never merely as means,* but always *at the same time as end in itself.* From this, however, arises a systematic combination of rational beings through communal objective laws, i.e. a realm, which, because these laws have as their aim the reference of these beings[d] to one

a. 1785: "Thus I will call this the principle of . . ."
b. The editors suggest 'jenem', which would translate: 'in contrast to that other, which . . .'
c. 1785: may
d. 1785: "as their aim their relation to one another . . ."

another as ends and means, can be called a 'realm of ends' (obviously only an ideal).[28]

But a rational being belongs as a *member* to the realm of ends if in this realm it gives universal law but is also itself subject to these laws. It belongs to it *as supreme head,* if as giving law it is subject to no will of another.[29]

[Ak 4:434] The rational being must always consider itself as giving law in a realm of ends possible through freedom of the will, whether as member or as supreme head. It can assert the place of the latter, however, not merely through the maxim of its will, but only when it is a fully independent being, without need and without limitation of faculties that are adequate to that will.

Morality thus consists in the reference of all action to that legislation through which alone a realm of ends is possible. But the legislation must be encountered in every rational being itself, and be able to arise from its will, whose principle therefore is: "Do no action in accordance with any other maxim, except one that could subsist with its being a universal law, and hence only so *that the will could through its maxim at the same time consider itself as universally legislative.*" Now if the maxims are not through their nature already necessarily in harmony with this objective principle of the rational beings, as universally legislative, then the necessity of the action in accordance with that principle is called 'practical necessitation', i.e. *duty.* Duty does not apply to the supreme head in the realm of ends, but it does to every member, and specifically, to all in equal measure.

The practical necessity of acting in accordance with this principle, i.e. duty, does not rest at all on feelings, impulses, or inclinations, but merely on the relation of rational beings to one another, in which the will of one rational being must always at the same time be considered as *universally legislative,* because otherwise the rational being could not think of the other rational beings as *ends in themselves.* Reason thus refers every maxim of the will as universally legislative to every other will and also to every action toward itself, and this not for the sake of any other practical motive or future advantage, but from the idea of the *dignity* of a rational being that obeys no law except that which at the same time it gives itself.

In the realm of ends everything has either a **price** or a **dignity**.[30] What has a price is such that something else can also be put in its place as its *equivalent;* by contrast, that which is elevated above all price, and admits of no equivalent, has a dignity.

That which refers to universal human inclinations and needs has a *market price;* that which, even without presupposing any need, is in accord
[Ak 4:435] with a certain taste, i.e. a satisfaction in the mere purposeless play of the

powers of our mind, an *affective price;* but that which constitutes the condition under which alone something can be an end in itself, does not have merely a relative worth, i.e. a price, but rather an inner worth, i.e. *dignity.* Now morality is the condition under which alone a rational being can be an end in itself, because only through morality is it possible to be a legislative member in the realm of ends. Thus morality and humanity, insofar as it is capable of morality, is that alone which has dignity. Skill and industry in labor have a market price; wit, lively imagination, and moods have an affective price; by contrast, fidelity in promising, benevolence from principle (not from instinct) have an inner worth. Lacking these principles, neither nature nor art contain anything that they could put in the place of them; for the worth of these principles does not consist in effects that arise from them, in the advantage and utility that they obtain, but rather in the dispositions, i.e. the maxims of the will, which in this way are ready to reveal themselves in actions, even if they are not favored with success. These actions also need no recommendation from any subjective disposition[a] or taste, regarding them with immediate favor and satisfaction, and no immediate propensity or feeling for it:[b] they exhibit the will that carries them out as an object of an immediate respect, for which nothing but reason is required in order to *impose* them on the will, not to *cajole* them from it *by flattery,* which latter would, in any event, be a contradiction in the case of duties. This estimation thus makes the worth of such a way of thinking to be recognized as dignity, and sets it infinitely far above all price, with which it cannot at all be brought into computation or comparison without, as it were, mistaking and assailing[c] its holiness.

And now, what is it that justifies the morally good disposition or virtue in making such high claims? It is nothing less than the *share* that it procures for the rational being *in the universal legislation,* thereby making it suitable as a member in a possible realm of ends, for which it by its own nature was already destined, as end in itself and precisely for this reason as legislative in the realm of ends, as free in regard to all natural laws, obeying only those that it gives itself and in accordance with which its maxims can belong to a universal legislation (to which it at the same time subjects   [Ak 4:436] itself). For nothing has a worth except that[d] which the law determines for

a. *Disposition*
b. *dieselbe,* which would appear to refer to 'morality'; some editors substitute the plural, so that this pronoun refers instead to 'these actions'
c. 'mistaking and assailing' = *vergreifen*
d. 1785: ". . . except the one the law determines"

it. The legislation itself, however, that determines all worth, must precisely for this reason have a dignity, i.e. an unconditioned, incomparable worth; the word *respect* alone yields a becoming expression for the estimation that a rational being must assign to it. *Autonomy* is thus the ground of the dignity of the human and of every rational nature.

The three ways mentioned of representing the principle of morality are, however, fundamentally only so many formulas of precisely the same law, one of which of itself unites the other two in itself.[31] Nonetheless, there is a variety among them, which is to be sure more subjectively than objectively practical,[a] namely, that of bringing an idea of reason nearer to intuition (in accordance with a certain analogy) and through this nearer to feeling. All maxims have, namely,

1) a *form,* which consists in universality, and then the formula of the moral imperative is expressed thus: "That the maxims must be chosen as if they are supposed to be valid as universal laws of nature";

2) a *matter,*[b] namely an end, and then the formula says: "That the rational being, as an end in accordance with its nature, hence as an end in itself, must serve for every maxim as a limiting condition of all merely relative and arbitrary ends";

3) *a complete determination*[32] of all maxims through that formula, namely: "That all maxims ought to harmonize from[c] one's own legislation into a possible realm of ends as a realm of nature."* A progression happens here, as through the categories of the *unity* of the form of the will (its universality), the *plurality* of the matter (the objects, i.e. the ends), and the *allness* or totality of the system of them.[33] But one does better in moral *judging* always to proceed in accordance with the strict method and take as ground the universal formula of the categorical imperative: *Act in accordance with that maxim which can at the same time make itself into a universal law.* But if one wants at the same time to obtain *access* for the moral law, then it is very useful to take one and the same action through the

[Ak 4:437]

a. This could also be translated as: '. . . more subjective than objectively practical'

b. Kant's text reads *Maxime;* but editors universally correct this to *Materie,* as seems absolutely required by the second sentence of 3) below.

c. 1785: as

[Ak 4:436]

*Teleology considers nature as a realm of ends, morality a possible realm of ends as a realm of nature. In the former, the realm of ends is a theoretical idea for the explanation of what exists. In the latter, it is a practical idea to bring about that which does not exist but what can become actual through our conduct [*Tun und Lassen*] and what we are to bring about in accord with precisely this idea.

three named concepts and thus, as far as may be done, to bring the action nearer to intuition.

Now we can end at the place from which we set out at the beginning, namely with the concept of an unconditionally good will. That *will* is *absolutely good* which cannot be evil, hence whose maxim, if it is made into a universal law, can never conflict with itself. This principle is therefore also its supreme law: "Act always in accordance with that maxim whose universality as law you can at the same time will"; this is the single condition under which a will can never be in conflict with itself, and such an imperative is categorical. Because the validity of the will as a universal law for possible actions has an analogy with the universal connection of the existence of things in accordance with universal laws, which is what is formal in nature in general, the categorical imperative can also be expressed thus: *Act in accordance with maxims that can at the same time have themselves as universal laws of nature for their object.* This, therefore, is the way the formula of an absolutely good will is constituted.

Rational nature discriminates itself from the rest in that it sets itself an end. This would be the matter of every good will. But since, in the idea of a will that is absolutely good without a limiting condition (of the attainment of this or that end), every end to be *effected* has to be thoroughly abstracted from (as it would make every will only relatively good), the end here has to be thought of not as an end to be effected *but as a self-sufficient* end, hence only negatively, i.e., never to be acted against, which therefore has to be estimated in every volition never merely as means but always at the same time as end. Now this cannot be other than the very subject of all possible ends, because this is at the same time the subject of a possible absolutely good will; for this will cannot without contradiction be set after any other object. The principle:[a] Accordingly, "act in reference to every rational being (to yourself and others) so that in your maxim it is always valid at the same time as an end in itself" is fundamentally the same as the principle "Act in accordance with a maxim that at the same time contains its own universal validity for every rational being." For that I ought to limit my [Ak 4:438] maxim in the use of means to every end to the condition of its universality as a law for every subject: this says just as much as that the subject of ends, i.e. the rational being itself, must be made the ground of all maxims of actions never merely as means, but as the supreme limiting condition in the use of all means, i.e. always at the same time as end.

a. 1785: "But the principle: . . ."

Now it incontestably follows from this that every rational being, as an end in itself, would have to be able to regard itself at the same time as universally legislative in regard to all laws to which it may be subject, because precisely this suitableness of its maxims for the universal legislation designates it as an end in itself, just as the fact that this dignity (prerogative) before all mere beings of nature brings with it to have to take its maxims always from its own point of view but also at the same time from that of every other rational being as a universally legislative being (which is why they are also called 'persons'). Now in such a way a world of rational beings (*mundus intelligibilis*)[a] is possible as a realm of ends, and specifically for all persons through their own legislation as members. Accordingly,[b] every rational being must act as if it were through its maxims always a legislative member in a universal realm of ends. The formal principle of these maxims is: "Act as though your maxim should serve at the same time as a universal law (for all rational beings)." A realm of ends is thus possible only in accordance with the analogy with a realm of nature, but only in accordance with maxims, i.e. with self-imposed rules, whereas the latter is possible only in accordance with laws of externally[c] necessitated efficient causes. Regardless of this, even though nature as a whole is regarded as a machine, nevertheless one also gives to it, insofar as it has reference to rational beings as its ends, on that ground, the name 'realm of nature'. Such a realm of ends would actually be brought about through maxims, the rule of which is prescribed by the categorical imperatives of all rational beings, *if they were universally followed.* Yet although the rational being might punctiliously follow these maxims himself, he cannot for that reason count on everyone else being faithful to them, nor on the realm of nature and its purposive order harmonizing with him, as a suitable member for a realm of ends that is possible through him, i.e. on its favoring his expectation of happiness; thus the law: "Act in accordance with maxims of a universally legislative member for a merely possible realm of ends" still remains in full force, because it commands categorically. And precisely in this lies the paradox that merely the dignity of humanity as rational nature, without any other end or advantage to be attained through it, hence the respect for a mere idea, ought nevertheless to serve as an unremitting precept of the will, and that the sublimity of the maxim consists in just its independence

a. intelligible world
b. 1785: "Nevertheless, . . ."
c. 1785: "laws also of externally . . ."

of all incentives, and the dignity of every rational subject consists in being a legislative member in the realm of ends; for otherwise it would have to be represented as subject only to the natural law of its needs. Although the natural realm too, as well as the realm of ends, is thought of as united under a supreme head, and the latter thereby would no longer remain a mere idea but obtain true reality, so that through this the maxim would receive the accretion of a strong incentive; yet no increase of its inner worth would thereby come about; for irrespective of that, this sole unlimited legislator must always be so represented as judging the worth of the rational beings only in accordance with their selfless conduct as prescribed by itself merely through that idea. The essence of things does not alter through their external relations, and it is in accordance with that which alone constitutes the absolute worth of the human being, without thinking about such relations, that he must be judged by whomever it may be, even by the highest being. *Morality* is thus the relation of actions to the autonomy of the will, that is, to the possible universal legislation through its maxims. That action which can subsist with the autonomy of the will, is *permitted;* that which does not agree with it, is *impermissible.* The will whose maxims necessarily harmonize with the laws of autonomy is a *holy,* absolutely good will. The dependence of a will which is not absolutely good on the principle of autonomy (moral necessitation) is *obligation.* Thus the latter cannot be referred to a holy being. The objective necessity of an action from obligation is called *duty.*

From what has just been said one can now easily explain how it is that although under the concept of duty we think a subjection to the law, we at the same time represent to ourselves a certain sublimity[34] and *dignity* in a person who fulfills all his duties. For to be sure, to the extent that the person is *subject* to the moral law, there is no sublimity in him, but there is to the extent that he is at the same time *legislative* in regard to this law, and is only for that reason subject to them. Also we have shown above how neither fear nor inclination, but solely respect for the law, is the incentive that can give the action its moral worth. Our own will, insofar as it would act only under the condition of a possible universal legislation through its maxims, this will possible to us in the idea, is the authentic object of respect, and the dignity of humanity consists precisely in this capacity for universal legislation, although with the proviso[a] that it is at the same time itself subject to this legislation.

[Ak 4:440]

a. *Beding*

Autonomy of the will
as the supreme principle of morality

Autonomy of the will is the property of the will through which it is a law to itself (independently of all properties of the objects of volition). The principle of autonomy is thus: "Not to choose otherwise than so that the maxims of one's choice are at the same time comprehended with it in the same volition as universal law." That this practical rule is an imperative, i.e. the will of every rational being is necessarily bound to it as a condition, cannot be proven through the mere analysis of the concepts occurring in it, because it is a synthetic proposition; one would have to advance beyond the cognition of objects and to a critique of the subject, i.e. of pure practical reason, since this synthetic proposition, which commands apodictically, must be able to be cognized fully *a priori;* but this enterprise does not belong in the present section. Yet that the specified principle of autonomy is the sole principle of morals, may well be established through the mere analysis of the concepts of morality. For thereby it is found that its principle must be a categorical imperative, but this commands neither more nor less than just this autonomy.

Heteronomy of the will
as the source of all ungenuine[a] principles of morality

If the will seeks that which should determine it *anywhere else* than in the suitability of its maxims for its own universal legislation, hence if it, insofar as it[b] advances beyond itself, seeks the law in the constitution of any of its objects, then *heteronomy* always comes out of this. Then the will does not give itself the law but the object through its relation to the will gives the law to it. Through this relation, whether it rests now on inclination or on representations of reason, only hypothetical imperatives are possible: "I ought to do something *because I will something else.*" By contrast, the moral, hence categorical, imperative says: "I ought to act thus-and-so even if I did not will anything else." E.g. the former one says: "I ought not to lie, if I want to retain my honorable reputation";[c] but the latter says: "I ought not to lie, even if I did not incur the least disgrace."[d] The last must therefore abstract from every object to the extent that it has no *influence* on the will, hence practical reason (will) does not merely administer some other interest, but merely proves its own commanding authority as supreme legisla-

a. *unechten*
b. 1785: "hence if it advances . . . , and seeks the law in . . ."
c. *bei Ehren bleiben*
d. *Schande*

tion. Thus, e.g. I should seek to promote someone else's happiness, not as if its existence mattered to me (whether through immediate inclination or any satisfaction indirectly through reason) but merely because the maxim that excludes it cannot be comprehended in one and the same volition as a universal law.

Division
of all possible principles of morality
from the
assumed fundamental concept of heteronomy

Here as elsewhere, human reason in its pure use, as long as it has gone without critique, has previously tried all possible incorrect routes before it succeeds in getting on the only true one.[35]

All principles that one may take from this point of view are either *empirical* or *rational*. The **first**, from the principle of *happiness*, are built on   [Ak 4:442] physical or moral feeling, the **second**, from the principle of *perfection*, are built either on the rational concept of it as a possible effect or on the concept of a self-sufficient perfection (the will of God) as determining cause of our will.[36]

Empirical principles are everywhere unsuited to having moral laws grounded on them. For the universality, with which they are to be valid for all rational beings without distinction, the unconditioned practical necessity, which is imposed on these beings through them, drops out if the ground of these principles is taken from the *particular adaptation of human nature* or from the contingent circumstances in which it is placed. Yet the principle of *one's own happiness* is most reprehensible, not merely because it is false and experience contradicts the pretense that one's own welfare always accords with conducting oneself well; also not merely because it contributes nothing to the grounding of morality, since making a happy human being is something other than making a good one, and making him prudent and sharp-witted for his own advantage is something other than making him virtuous; but rather because it attributes incentives to morality that would sooner undermine it and annihilate its entire sublimity, since they put the motivations for virtue in the same class as those for vice and only teach us to draw better calculations, but utterly extinguish the specific difference between them; by contrast, moral feeling, this allegedly special sense* (however shallow the appeal to it may be, since those who

---

*I count the principle of moral feeling to that of happiness, because every em-   [Ak 4:442] pirical interest promises a contribution to welfare through the agreeableness some

cannot *think* believe they can help themselves out by *feeling* when it comes to universal laws, even though feelings, which by nature are infinitely distinguished from one another in degree, cannot yield an equal standard of good and evil, nor can one validly judge for others at all through his feeling) nevertheless remains closer to morality and its dignity by showing virtue the honor of ascribing to it *immediately* the satisfaction and esteem we have for it, and not saying directly to its face, as it were, that it is not its beauty, but only our advantage, that attaches us to it.

Among *rational* grounds[a] of morality, the ontological concept of *perfection* (however empty, indeterminate hence unusable it may be for finding in the immeasurable field of possible reality the greatest suitable sum for us, and however much it has an unavoidable propensity to turn in a circle in order to distinguish the reality talked about here specifically from every other, and cannot avoid covertly presupposing the morality it ought to explain) is nevertheless better than the theological concept, of deriving morality from a divine all-perfect will, not merely because we do not intuit his perfection, but can derive it solely from our concepts, of which morality is the foremost one, but because if we do not do this (which, if we did, would be a crude circle in explanation), the concept of his will that is left over to us, the attributes[b] of the desire for glory and domination, bound up with frightful representations of power and vengeance, would have to make a foundation for a system of morals that is directly opposed to morality.

But if I had to choose between the concept of moral sense and that of perfection in general (both of which at least do not infringe morality, even if they are not at all suitable for supporting it as a foundation), then I would determine myself for the latter, because, since it at least transfers the decision of the question from sensibility to the court of pure reason, even if here it decides nothing, nevertheless it preserves unfalsified the indeterminate idea (of a will good in itself) for closer determination.

Besides, I believe I can dispense with an extensive refutation of all these doctrines. It is so easy, and even those whose office it is to declare themselves for one of these theories presumably have such good insight into it (because their hearers would not tolerate a postponement of judgment),

---

thing affords, whether this happens immediately and without any aim to advantage or in regard to the latter. Likewise one must, with *Hutcheson,* count the principle of sympathetic participation in another's happiness under the same moral sense assumed by him.

a. *rationalen oder Vernunftgründe*
b. *Eigenschaften*

that it would be only superfluous labor. What interests us more here is to know that these principles everywhere set up nothing but heteronomy of the will as the first ground of morality and just for this reason must necessarily miscarry regarding their end.

Wherever an object of the will has to be taken as the ground in order [Ak 4:444] to prescribe the rule determining that will, there the rule is nothing but heteronomy; the imperative is conditioned, namely: *if* or *because* one wills this object, one ought to act thus or so; hence it can never command morally, i.e. categorically. Now the object may determine the will by means of inclination, as with the principle of one's own happiness, or by means of a reason directed to objects of our possible volition in general, in the principle of perfection; then the will never determines itself *immediately* through the representation of the action, but only through the incentive, which the foreseen effect of the action has on the will; *I ought to do something because I will something other than that,* and another law in my subject must therefore be taken as ground, in accordance with which I necessarily will this other thing, which law once again needs an imperative that limits this maxim. For because the impulse that the representation of an object possible through our powers is supposed to exercise on the subject's will in accordance with its natural constitution, whether it be of sensibility (of inclination and taste) or of understanding and reason—which, in accordance with the particular adaptation of its nature, that faculty exercises with satisfaction in an object ᵃ—it is really nature that would give the law, which as such would have to be not only cognized and proven through experience, and hence is in itself contingent and thereby becomes unsuitable for an apodictic rule such as the moral rule has to be; but it is *always only heteronomy* of the will, the will does not give the law to itself, but rather an alien impulse gives it by means of the subject's nature, which is attuned to the receptiveness of the will.

The absolutely good will, whose principle must be a categorical imperative, will therefore, undetermined in regard to all objects, contain merely the *form of volition* in general, and indeed as autonomy, i.e. the suitability of the maxim of every good will to make itself into a universal law is itself the sole law that the will of every rational being imposes on itself, without grounding it on any incentive or interest in it.

How such a synthetic practical proposition a priori *is possible,* and why it is necessary, is a problem whose solution no longer lies within the

---

a. 1785: "reason takes in perfection in general, (whose existence either from itself or only depending on the highest self-sufficient perfection), . . ."

boundaries of the metaphysics of morals, neither have we here asserted   [Ak 4:d
its truth, much less pretended to have a proof of it in our control. We
showed only, through the development of the generally accepted concept
of morality,[a] that an autonomy of the will is unavoidably attached to that
concept of the will, or rather is its ground. Thus whoever takes morality
to be something, and not a chimerical idea without truth, must at the same
time concede the stated principle of it. This section, therefore, like the first
one, was merely analytical. Now that morality is no figment of the mind,
which follows if the categorical imperative, and with it autonomy of the
will, is true and absolutely necessary as a principle *a priori*—this requires
a *possible synthetic use of pure practical reason,* upon which, however, we
may not venture without preceding it with a *critique* of this very faculty of
reason, which we have to exhibit in the last section as the main feature of
this critique in a way sufficient for our aim.

a. *allgemein im Schwange gehenden Begriffs der Sittlichkeit*

Third section

Transition
from the metaphysics of morals
to the critique of pure practical reason

The concept of freedom
is the key to the definition[a] of autonomy of the will.

The *will* is a species of causality of living beings, insofar as they are rational, and *freedom* would be that quality of this causality by which it can be effective independently of alien causes *determining* it; just as *natural necessity* is the quality of the causality of all beings lacking reason, of being determined to activity through the influence of alien causes.

The proposed definition[b] of freedom is *negative,* and hence unfruitful in affording insight into its essence; yet from it flows a *positive* concept of freedom, which is all the more rich in content and more fruitful. Since the concept of a causality carries with it that of *laws* in accordance with which must be posited, through that which we call a cause, something else, namely its result; therefore freedom, even though it is not a quality of the will in accordance with natural laws, is not for this reason lawless, but rather it has to be a causality in accordance with unchangeable laws, but of a particular kind; for otherwise a free will would be an impossibility.[c] Natural necessity was a heteronomy of efficient causes; for every effect was possible only in accordance with the law that something else determined the efficient cause to causality; what else, then, could the freedom of the [Ak 4:447] will be, except autonomy, i.e. the quality of the will of being a law to itself? But the proposition: "The will is in all actions a law to itself," designates only the principle of acting in accordance with no other maxim than that which can also have itself as a universal law as its object. But this is just the formula of the categorical imperative and the principle of morality: thus a free will and a will under moral laws are the same.

Thus if freedom of the will is presupposed, then morality, together with its principle, follows from this, through the mere analysis of its concept.

a. *Erklärung*
b. *Erklärung*
c. *Unding*

Nonetheless, the latter is always a synthetic proposition: an absolutely good will is that whose maxim can always contain itself considered as universal law, for through analysis of the concept of an absolutely good will that quality of the maxim cannot be found. Such synthetic propositions, however, are possible only when both cognitions are combined with one another through the connection with a third in which they are both to be encountered.[1] The *positive* concept of freedom makes for[a] this third, which cannot be, as with physical causes, the nature of the world of sense (in whose concept the concepts of something as cause comes together in relation to *something else* as effect). What this third thing must be, to which freedom points and of which we have an idea *a priori,* still cannot be directly indicated here, and to make comprehensible the deduction of the concept of freedom from pure practical reason, with it also the possibility of a categorical imperative, instead still needs some preparation.

Freedom must be presupposed
as a quality of the will of all rational beings.

It is not enough that we ascribe freedom to our will, on whatever grounds, if we do not also have sufficient grounds to attribute the same quality also to all rational beings. For since morality serves as a law for us merely as for *rational beings,* it must also be valid for all rational beings, and since it must be derived solely from the quality of freedom, therefore freedom must also be proved as a quality of the will of all rational beings, and it is

not enough to establish it from certain alleged experiences of human nature (although this is absolutely impossible, and it can be established solely *a priori*); but rather one must prove it of the activity of rational beings in general, who are endowed with a will. Now I say: Every being that cannot act otherwise than *under the idea of freedom,* is precisely for this reason actually free in a practical respect, i.e. all laws inseparably combined with freedom are valid for it, just as if its will had also been declared[b] free in itself and in a way that is valid in theoretical philosophy.* Now I assert that we must necessarily lend to every rational being that has a will also the idea

a. *schafft*
b. *erklärt*

*I take this route, of assuming freedom as sufficient for our aim only as rational beings ground it *on the idea* in their actions, so that I may not be obligated to prove freedom also in its theoretical intent. For even if this latter is left unsettled, these same laws that would obligate a being that is actually free are still valid for a being that cannot act otherwise than as under the idea of its own freedom. Thus we can free ourselves of the burden that pressures theory.

of freedom, under which alone it would act. For in such a being we think a reason that is practical, i.e. has causality in regard to its objects. Now one cannot possibly think a reason that, in its own consciousness, would receive steering from elsewhere in regard to its judgments; for then the subject would ascribe the determination of its power of judgment not to its reason but to an impulse. It must regard itself as the author of its principles independently of alien influences, consequently it must, as practical reason or as the will of a rational being, be regarded by itself as free, i.e. the will of a rational being can be a will of its own only under the idea of freedom and must therefore with a practical aim be attributed to all rational beings.

Of the interest attaching to the ideas of morality

We have ultimately traced the determined concept of morality to the idea of freedom; but we cannot prove this freedom as something actual, not even in ourselves, nor in human nature; we saw only that we have to   [Ak 4:449] presuppose it if we would think of a being as rational and as endowed with consciousness of its causality in regard to actions, i.e. with a will; thus we find that from precisely the same ground we have to attribute to every being endowed with reason and will this quality, to determine itself to action under the idea of its freedom.

From the presupposition of these ideas,[a] however, there also flowed the consciousness of a law of acting: that the subjective principles of actions, i.e. maxims, have always to be taken so that they can also be valid objectively, i.e. universally as principles, hence serve for our own universal legislation. But why ought I to subject myself to this principle, and specifically as a rational being in general, hence through this also all other beings endowed with reason? I will concede that no interest *drives* me to it, for that would yield no categorical imperative; but I must necessarily *take* an interest in it, and gain insight into how that happens to be; for this 'ought' is really a volition that would be valid for every rational being, under the condition that reason were practical in him without any hindrances; for beings, such as we are, who are also affected through sensibility, as with incentives of another kind, with whom what reason for itself alone would always do does not always happen, that necessity of action is called only an[b] 'ought', and the subjective necessity is different from the objective.

---

a. *diese Ideen*, which seems to refer to the "ideas of morality" mentioned in the subheading. Because this yields a doubtful meaning for the sentence, some editors amend the text to read *diese Idee* (sc. the idea of freedom).
  b. 1785: "in the"

It therefore appears as if in the idea of freedom we really only presupposed the moral law, namely the principle of the autonomy of the will itself, and could not prove its reality and objective necessity for itself; and then we would still have gained something quite considerable, more than would have happened otherwise, by at least determining the genuine principle more precisely, but in regard to its validity and the practical necessity of subjecting ourselves to it, we would have come no further; for to someone who asked us why the universal validity of our maxim as a law has to be the limiting condition of our actions, and on what we ground the worth that we attribute to this way of acting—a worth that is to be so great that there can nowhere be any higher interest—and how it happens to be [Ak 4:450] that the human being believes he feels his personal worth through it alone, and that over against it an agreeable or disagreeable condition is held to be nothing—to him we can give no satisfactory answer.

We indeed find that we can take an interest in a constitution of personality[a] that carries with it no interest at all in the condition, if only the former makes us susceptible to partaking in the latter just in case reason should effect the distribution of it, i.e. that the mere worthiness of being happy, even without the motive to partake in this happiness, could interest for itself: but this judgment is in fact only the effect of moral laws whose importance has already been presupposed (if we separate ourselves from all empirical interest through the idea of freedom), but that we ought to separate ourselves from this, i.e. consider ourselves as free in acting and thus nevertheless take ourselves to be subject to certain laws in order to find a worth merely in our person, and that this could compensate us for the loss of all the worth procured for our condition; and how this is possible, thus *from whence the moral law obligates*—in such a way we still gain no insight into this.

One must freely admit it[b] that a kind of circle shows itself here, from which, it seems, there is no way out. In the order of efficient causes we assume ourselves to be free in order to think of ourselves as under moral laws in the order of ends, and then afterward we think of ourselves as subject to these laws because we have attributed freedom of the will to ourselves, for freedom and the will giving its own laws are both autonomy, hence reciprocal concepts, of which, however, just for this reason, one cannot be used to define[c] the other and provide the ground for it, but at most only with a logical intent to bring various apparent representations of the same object

---

a. *persönliche Beschaffenheit*
b. This word added in 1786
c. *erklären,* which could also be translated 'explain'

to a single concept (as different fractions with the same value are brought to the lowest common denominator).

But one way out remains for us, namely to seek whether, when we think of ourselves through freedom as *a priori* efficient causes, we do not take a different standpoint from when we represent ourselves in accordance with our actions as effects that we see before our eyes.

No subtle reflection is required to make the following remark, but rather one can assume that the commonest understanding might make it, even if in its own way, through an obscure distinction of the power of judgment [Ak 4:451] that it calls feeling: that all representations that come to us without our choice (like those of sense) give us objects to cognize only as they affect us, so that what they might be in themselves remains unknown to us; hence that as regards this species of representations, even with the most strenuous attention and distinctness that the understanding might add to them, we can attain merely to the cognition of *appearances*, never to *things in themselves*.[2] As soon as this distinction is made (perhaps merely through the variation noted between the representations that are given to us from somewhere else, in which we are passive, and those which we produce solely from ourselves, and thus prove our activity), then it follows of itself that one must concede and assume behind the appearances something else that is not appearance, namely the things in themselves, even if of ourselves we are satisfied that since they never can become known to us except as they affect us, we can never come any nearer to them and can never know what they are in themselves. This[a] must yield a distinction, although a crude one, of a *world of sense* from a *world of understanding*,[3] of which the first, in accordance with the variations in sensibility of many ways of contemplating the world, can also be extremely varied, whereas the second, on which it is grounded, always remains the same. Even about himself and in accordance with the acquaintance that the human being has of himself through inner sensation, he may not presume to cognize how he is in himself. For since he does not, as it were, make himself and gets his concept not *a priori* but empirically, it is natural that he can take in information even about himself through inner sense and consequently only through the appearance of his nature and the way his consciousness is affected, whereas he necessarily assumes about this constitution of his own subject, which is composed of sheer appearances, that it is grounded on something else, namely his I, however that may be constituted in itself, and must therefore count himself in regard to mere perception and the receptivity of sensations as in

a. 1785: "They must yield . . ."

the *world of sense,* but in regard to whatever in him may be pure activity (what attains to consciousness not through the affection of the senses but immediately), he must count himself as in the *intellectual world,* of which, however, he has no further acquaintance.

A reflective human being must draw such a conclusion about all things that might come before him; presumably it is also to be encountered in the commonest understanding, which, as is well known, is very much inclined to expect behind the objects of sense always something invisible and for itself active, but is corrupted by the fact that it wants to make this invisible once again into something sensible, i.e. into an object of intuition, and thereby does not become by any degree the wiser.[a]

Now the human being actually finds in himself a faculty through which he distinguishes himself from all other things, and even from himself insofar as he is affected by objects, and this is *reason.* This as pure self-activity is elevated even above the *understanding* in the respect that although the latter is also self-activity and does not, like sense, contain mere representations that arise only when one is affected by things (hence passive), it can produce no other concepts from its activity except those that merely serve to *bring sensible representations under rules* and thereby to unite them in one consciousness, without which use of sensibility it would think nothing at all,[4] while by contrast, reason, under the name of the ideas, shows such a pure spontaneity that it thereby goes far beyond everything that sensibility can provide it, and proves its most excellent occupation by distinguishing the world of the senses and the world of the understanding from one another, thereby, however, delineating the limits of the understanding itself.[5]

On account of this, a rational being has to regard itself *as an intelligence* (thus not from the side of its lower powers), as belonging not to the world of sense but to the world of understanding; hence it has two standpoints, from which it can consider itself and cognize the laws for the use of its powers, consequently all its actions: *first,* insofar as it belongs to the world of sense, under natural laws (heteronomy), and *second,* as belonging to the intelligible world, under laws which are independent of nature, not empirical, but rather grounded merely in reason.

As a rational being, hence one belonging to the intelligible world, the human being can never think of the causality of its own will otherwise than under the idea of freedom; for independence of determinate[b] causes

[Ak 4:452]

a. *klüger*

b. *bestimmten;* following Kant's formulation later at Ak 4:455, editors often emend this to *bestimmenden* ('determining') of the world of sense (such as reason must always attribute to itself) is freedom. Now with the idea of freedom the concept of *autonomy* is inseparably bound up, but with the latter the universal principle of morality, which in the idea grounds all actions of *rational* beings just as the natural law grounds all appearances.

Now the suspicion has been removed that we aroused above, that there [Ak 4:453] was a hidden circle contained in our inference from freedom to autonomy and from the latter to the moral law, namely, that we perhaps took freedom as a ground only for the sake of the moral law in order afterward to infer the latter once again from freedom, hence that we could not offer any ground for the former, but rather only as begging a question,[a] which well-disposed souls might concede to us, but which we could never set up as a provable proposition. For now we see that if we think of ourselves as free, then we transport ourselves as members into the world of understanding and cognize the autonomy of the will, together with its[b] consequence, morality; but if we think of ourselves as obligated by duty,[c] then we consider ourselves as belonging to the world of sense and yet at the same time to the world of understanding.

How is a categorical imperative possible?

The rational being counts himself as intelligence in the world of understanding, and merely as an efficient cause belonging to this world does it call its causality a *will*. From the other side, however, it is conscious of itself also as a piece of the world of sense, in which its actions, as mere appearances of that causality are encountered, but whose possibility from the latter, with which we have no acquaintance, is something into which we can have no insight, but rather in place of that we have to have insight into those actions as determined through other appearances, namely desires and inclinations as belonging to the world of sense. As a mere member of the world of understanding, all my actions would be perfectly in accord with the principle of the autonomy of the pure will; as a mere piece of the sensible world, they would have to be taken as entirely in accord with the natural law of desires and inclinations, hence with the heteronomy of nature. (The former would rest on the supreme principle of morality, the second

a. *sondern nur als Erbittung eines Prinzips.* If there is a verb in this clause, it is not obvious what it is; the clause might refer by parallel construction to *aufstellen könnten* ('could set up') in the following clause.

b. 1785: *seiner,* the most natural grammatical referent of which would have to be 'will'; 1786 changes this to *ihrer,* whose natural referent is 'autonomy'

c. *verpflichtet*

on that of happiness.) But because[a] *the world of understanding contains the ground of the world of sense, hence also of its laws,* hence is immediately legislative in regard to my will (which belongs wholly to the world of understanding), and hence must also be thought of wholly as such, therefore as intelligence I will cognize myself, although on the other side as a being belonging to the world of sense, as nevertheless subject to the laws of the first, i.e. to reason, which in the idea of freedom contains the law of the understanding's world, and thus to autonomy of the will; consequently I must regard the laws of the world of understanding for myself as imperatives and the actions that accord with this principle as duties.

[Ak 4:454]

And thus categorical imperatives are possible through the fact that the idea of freedom makes me into a member of an intelligible world, through which, if I were that alone, all my actions *would* always be in accord with the autonomy of the will, but since I intuit myself at the same time as member of the world of sense, they *ought* to be in accord with it, which *categorical* 'ought' represents a synthetic proposition a priori by the fact that to my will affected through sensible desires there is also added the idea of precisely the same will, but one belonging to the world of understanding, a pure will, practical for itself, that contains the supreme condition of the first in accordance with reason; it is approximately in this way that concepts of the understanding, which for themselves signify nothing but lawful form in general, are added to intuitions of the world of sense and through that make possible synthetic propositions a priori on which rests all cognition of a nature.[6]

The practical use of common human reason confirms the correctness of this deduction. There is no one, even the most wicked scoundrel, if only he is otherwise accustomed to use his reason, who does not wish, if one lays before him examples of honesty in aims, steadfastness in following good maxims, sympathetic participation, and general benevolence (and in addition combined with great sacrifices of advantage and convenience) that he might also be so disposed. But he cannot bring it about on account of his inclinations and impulses, while at the same time he wishes to be free of such burdensome inclinations. Thus through this he proves that with a will free of the impulses of sensibility, he transports himself in thoughts into entirely another order of things than that of his desires in the field of sensibility, since from that wish he can expect no gratification of desires, hence no condition that would satisfy any of his actual or even thinkable inclinations (for then the very idea that entices him to the wish would forfeit its

a. In 1785 these two words were emphasized along with what follows them.

superiority), but he can expect only a greater inner worth of his person. This better person, however, he believes himself to be when he transports [Ak 4:455] himself into the standpoint of a member of the world of understanding, to which the idea of freedom, i.e. independence^a of *determining* causes of the sensible world, involuntarily necessitates him, and in which he is conscious of a good will, which constitutes by his own admission the law for his evil will as a member of the sensible world, the law with whose authority he becomes acquainted when he transgresses it. The moral 'ought' is thus his own necessary volition as a member of an intelligible world and is thought of him as an 'ought' only insofar as he at the same time considers himself as a member of the sensible world.

Of the uttermost boundary of all practical philosophy
All human beings think of themselves, regarding the will, as free. Hence all judgments about actions come as if they *ought* to have *happened* even if they *have not happened.* Yet this freedom is no experiential concept, and also cannot be one, because freedom always remains even though experience shows the opposite of those requirements that are represented as necessary under the presupposition of freedom. On the other side it is just as necessary that everything that happens should remain unexceptionably determined in accordance with natural laws, and this natural necessity is also not an experiential concept, precisely because it carries with it the concept of necessity, hence of a cognition *a priori.* But this concept of a nature is confirmed through experience and must unavoidably be presupposed if experience, i.e. cognition of objects of sense connected in accordance with universal laws, is to be possible. Hence freedom is only an *idea* of reason, whose objective reality is doubtful in itself, but nature is a *concept of understanding* that proves its reality from examples in experience and necessarily must prove it.

Now although from this arises a dialectic of reason, since in regard to the will the freedom attributed to it appears to stand in contradiction with natural necessity;⁷ and at this fork in the road, with a *speculative intent,* reason finds the route of natural necessity much more traveled and useful than that of freedom: yet with a *practical intent* the footpath of freedom is the only one on which it is possible to make use of one's reason in conduct;^b hence it is just as impossible for the subtlest philosophy as [Ak 4:456] for the commonest human reason to ratiocinate freedom away. Thus the

a. 1785: ". . . to which the idea of freedom from determining causes . . ."
b. *Tun und Lassen*

latter[a] must presuppose that no true contradiction is encountered between freedom and the natural necessity of precisely the same human actions, for it can give up the concept of nature just as little as it can that of freedom.

Nevertheless this seeming contradiction must be done away with at least in a convincing way, even if one could never conceive how freedom is possible. For if even the thought of freedom contradicts itself or the thought of nature, which is just as necessary, then it, as opposed to natural necessity, had to be[b] completely given up.

But it is impossible to escape this contradiction if the subject, which supposes itself free, were to think itself *in the same sense* or *in precisely the same relations* when it calls itself free as when it assumes it is subject to the natural law in regard to that very action. Hence it is an unremitting problem of speculative philosophy to show at least that its deception of a contradiction rests on the fact that we think of the human being in another sense and in other relations when we call him free than when we take him, as a piece of nature, to be subject to its law, and that both not only *can* very well stand side by side, but also that they have to be thought *as necessarily united* in the same subject, since otherwise no ground can be supplied why we should burden reason with an idea that, even if it can be united *without contradiction* with another that is satisfactorily confirmed, yet nevertheless involves us in an enterprise in which reason in its theoretical use is put in a very tight spot. This duty, however, lies merely on speculative philosophy, so that it can free the way for practical philosophy. Thus it is not put at the discretion of the philosopher whether he will remove this seeming conflict or leave it untouched; for in the latter case the theory about it is *bonum vacans,*[c] and the fatalist can with grounds enter into possession of it and expel all morals from its supposed property as taken possession of without title.

Yet one can still not say that the boundary of practical philosophy begins here. For the settlement of that contest does not at all belong to it, but rather it only demands of speculative reason that it should bring to an end the disunity in which these theoretical questions involve it, so that practical reason can have tranquillity and security against external attacks that might contest the terrain on which it wants to build.

[Ak 4:457]

a. *Diese*, which apparently refers to 'the commonest human reason', but in the context of the entire paragraph could conceivably be taken to refer to 'reason' in the earlier part of the sentence

b. *mußte*; some editors read *müßte*, 'would have to be'

c. 'vacant good', i.e., a piece of property belonging to no one

But the legal claim,[a] even of common human reason, on freedom of the will, is grounded on the consciousness and the admitted presupposition of the independence of reason from all merely subjectively determined causes, which together constitute that which belongs merely to sensation, hence under the general term 'sensibility'. The human being, who in such a wise considers himself as an intelligence, sets himself thereby in another order of things, and in a relation to determinate grounds of an entirely different kind, when he thinks of himself as an intelligence with a will, consequently as endowed with causality, than when he perceives himself as a phenomenon in the world of sense (which he actually is too), and subjects his causality, regarding external determination, to natural laws. Now he soon becomes aware that both can take place at the same time, indeed even that they must. For that a *thing in its appearance* (belonging to the world of sense) is subject to certain laws, of which the very same thing *as thing* or being *in itself* is independent, contains not the least contradiction; but that he must represent and think of himself in this twofold way rests, regarding the first, on the consciousness of himself as an object affected through sense, and as far as the second goes, on the consciousness of himself as intelligence, i.e. as independent in his use of reason of sensible impressions (hence as belonging to the world of understanding).

Hence it comes about that the human being presumes to claim a will that lets nothing be put to its account that belongs merely to its desires and inclinations, and on the contrary thinks of actions through itself as possible, or indeed even as necessary, that can happen only by disregarding all desires and sensible stimuli. The causality of these actions lies in him as intelligence and in the laws of the effects and actions in accordance with principles of an intelligible world, of which he perhaps knows nothing further except that there it is solely reason, and indeed a reason that is pure and independent of sensibility, that gives the law, and likewise, since in that world he himself only as intelligence is the authentic self (as human being, by contrast, only appearance of himself), those laws apply to him immediately and categorically, so that whatever inclinations and impulses (hence the entire nature of the world of sense) stimulates him to, they cannot infringe the laws of his volition as intelligence, even that he is not responsible to the first and does not ascribe it to his authentic self, i.e. his will, though he does ascribe to it the indulgence that it would like to bear [Ak 4:458]

a. *Rechtsanspruch*

toward them, if, to the disadvantage of the rational laws of the will, he were to concede them influence on its maxims.[a]

Through the fact that practical reason *thinks* itself into a world of understanding, it does not overstep its boundaries, but it would if it tried to *intuit* or *sense* itself *into it*.[b] The former is only a negative thought, in regard to the world of sense, which gives no laws to reason in determination of the will, and is only in this single point positive that that freedom, as a negative determination, is at the same time combined with a (positive) faculty and even with a causality of reason, which we call a 'will', so to act that the principle of the actions is in accord with the essential constitution of a rational cause, i.e. the condition of the universal validity of the maxim as a law. If, however, it were to fetch an *object of the will*, i.e. a motivation, from the world of understanding, then it would overstep its boundaries and presume to be acquainted with something of which it knows nothing. The concept of a world of the understanding is therefore only a *standpoint*, apart from appearances, which reason sees itself necessitated to take *in order to think of itself as practical*, which, if the influences of sensibility were determining for the human being, would not be possible, but which is necessary insofar as his consciousness of himself as intelligence, hence as a cause that is rational and active through reason, i.e. freely efficient, is not to be renounced. This thought obviously carries with it the idea of another order and legislation than that of the natural mechanism that pertains to the world of sense, and makes necessary the concept of an intelligible world (i.e. the whole of rational beings as things in themselves), but without the least presumption here to think of them further than merely as regards their *formal* condition, i.e. the universality of the maxim of the will, as law, hence the autonomy of the latter,[c] which alone can subsist with freedom; whereas on the contrary, all laws that are determined to an object, give heteronomy, which is encountered only in natural laws and can also pertain only to the world of sense.

a. In this sentence, it is unclear whether some of the pronouns refer to 'the human being' or to 'his will'. The present translation assumes the latter. Taking the former, the end of the sentence would read: "... i.e. his will, though he does ascribe to himself the indulgence he would like to bear toward them if, to the disadvantage of the rational laws of the will, he were to concede them influence on his maxims."

b. *wenn sie sich hineinschauen, hineinempfinden wollte*

c. *als Gesetze, mithin der Autonomie des letzteren*; the referent of the last term would have to be 'will' (singular), but the apparent antecedent is plural. Some editors therefore amend *Gesetze* to *Gesetz*, or else to *Gesetzes* (genitive singular), making the sentence end '[the law's] autonomy'.

But then reason would overstep all its boundaries if it undertook to *explain how* pure reason could be practical, which would be fully the same as [Ak 4:459] the problem of explaining *how freedom is possible.*

For we can explain nothing unless we can trace it back to laws the object of which can be given in some possible experience. But freedom is a mere idea, whose objective reality can in no wise be established in accordance with natural laws, hence also not in any possible experience; for the same reason, because no example may ever be attributed to freedom itself in accordance with any analogy, freedom can never be comprehended nor even can insight into it be gained. It is valid only as a necessary presupposition of reason in a being that believes itself to be conscious of a will, i.e. of a faculty varying from a mere faculty of desire (namely, of determining itself to action as an intelligence, hence in accordance with laws of reason, independently of natural instincts). But where the determination in accordance with natural laws ceases, there too ceases all *explanation,* and there is nothing left over except *defense,* i.e. aborting the objections of those who pretend to have looked deeper into the essence of things and therefore brazenly declare[a] freedom to be impossible. One can only show them that the presumed contradiction they have found in it lies elsewhere, since in order to make the natural law valid in regard to human actions, they necessarily have to consider the human being as appearance, and now when one demands of them that they should also think of him as intelligence, also[b] as thing in itself, they are still considering him as appearance, to which obviously the separation of his causality (i.e. of his will) from all natural laws of the world of sense in one and the same subject would stand in contradiction, but that contradiction goes away if they would keep in mind, and even admit, as is only fair,[c] that behind appearances things in themselves (although hidden) must ground them, and one cannot demand of their effective laws that they should be the same as those under which their appearances stand.

The subjective impossibility of *explaining*[d] the freedom of the will is the same as the impossibility of bringing to light and making comprehensible an *interest** that the human being could take in moral laws; and neverthe- [Ak 4:460] less he actually does take an interest in them, the foundation of which in us

a. *erklären*; so the clause could also be translated, ". . . brazenly explain freedom to be impossible" or ". . . brazenly define freedom to be impossible"

b. 1785: "as intelligence, but as . . ."

c. *billig*

d. *erklären*, which could also be translated here as 'defining'

*'Interest' is that through which reason becomes practical, i.e. becomes a cause [Ak 4:459] determining the will. Hence one says only of a rational being that it takes an interest

we call 'moral feeling', which is falsely given out by some as the standard of our moral judgment, since it has to be regarded rather as the *subjective* effect that the law exercises on the will, for which reason alone provides the objective grounds.

In order for a sensibly affected rational being to will that which reason alone prescribes the 'ought', there obviously must belong to it a faculty of reason to *instill* a *feeling of pleasure* or satisfaction in the fulfillment of duty, hence a causality of reason to determine sensibility in accordance with its principles. It is entirely impossible, however, to gain insight, i.e. to make comprehensible *a priori,* how a mere thought that contains nothing sensible in it, would produce a sensation of pleasure or displeasure; for that is a particular kind of causality, of which, as of all causality, we can determine nothing at all *a priori,* but rather we have to ask experience alone about it. But since experience can provide no relation of cause to effect except that between two objects of experience, but here pure reason, through mere ideas (which yield no object at all for experience), ought to be the cause of an effect which obviously lies in experience, it is entirely impossible for us human beings to have an explanation how and why the *universality of the maxim as a law,* hence morality, should interest us. Only this much is certain: that it does not have validity for us *because it interests* us (for that is heteronomy and dependency of practical reason on sensibility, [Ak 4:461]   namely a feeling grounding it, which could never be morally legislative), but rather that it interests us because it is valid for us as human beings, since it has arisen from our will as intelligence, hence from our authentic self; *but what belongs to the mere appearance is necessarily subordinated by reason to the constitution of the thing in itself.*

Thus the question, 'How is a categorical imperative possible?' can be answered to this extent: one can state the sole presupposition under which alone it is possible, namely the idea of freedom, and to the extent that one can have insight into the necessity of this presupposition, which is sufficient for the *practical use* of reason, i.e. for the conviction of the *validity*

[Ak 4:460]   in something; creatures without reason only feel sensible impulses. Reason takes an immediate interest in an action only when the universal validity of its maxim is a sufficient determining ground of the will. Such an interest is alone pure. But if it can determine the will only by means of another object of desire or under the presupposition of a particular feeling of the subject, then reason takes only a mediated interest in the action, and since reason for itself alone without experience can bring to light neither objects of the will nor a feeling grounding it, the latter interest would be only empirical and not a pure rational interest. The logical interest of reason (to promote its insights) is never immediate but presupposes aims of its use.

of this imperative, hence also of the moral law; but how this presupposition itself is possible, no insight into that can be gained through any human reason. Under the presupposition of freedom of the will, its *autonomy,* as the formal condition under which alone it can be determined, is a necessary consequence. To presuppose this freedom of the will is also not only (as speculative philosophy can show) entirely *possible* (without falling into contradiction to the principle of natural necessity in the connection of appearances in the world of sense), but it is also without any further condition *necessary* to impute[a] to it practically all its voluntary[b] actions, i.e. necessary as condition in the idea, to a rational being, who is conscious of its causality through reason, hence of its will (which is distinguished from desires). But now *how* pure reason can for itself be practical, without any other incentive that might be taken from anywhere else, i.e. how the mere *principle of the universal validity of all its maxims as laws* (which obviously would be the form of a pure practical reason), without any material (object) of the will in which one might previously take any interest, should for itself yield an incentive and effect an interest that would be called purely *moral*—or in other words, *how pure reason could be practical*—all human reason is entirely incapable of explaining that, and all the effort and labor spent in seeking an explanation is lost.

It is precisely the same as if I sought to get to the ground of how freedom itself, as the causality of a will, is possible. For there I forsake the philosophical ground of explanation and have no other. Now of course I [Ak 4:462] could enthuse about[c] in the intelligible world that is left over to me, in the world of intelligences; but although I have an *idea* of it, which has its own good ground, I still have not the least *acquaintance* with it and also can never reach one through every striving of my natural faculty of reason. It signifies only a 'something' that is left over if I have excluded everything from the determining grounds of my will that belongs to the world of sense, merely in order to limit the principle of motivation from the field of sensibility, by setting boundaries to it and showing that it does not embrace all in all, but that outside that principle I am still more; but I am not any further acquainted with this 'more'. Of pure reason, which thinks this ideal, there is left over to me to be thought, after the separation of all matter, i.e. the cognition of objects, only the form, namely the practical law of the universal validity of maxims, and in accord with this, reason in reference to a pure world of understanding as possible efficient cause, i.e. as determining

a. *unterzulegen*
b. *willkürlich*
c. *herumschwärmen*

the will; here the incentive has to be entirely lacking; it would have to be this idea of an intelligible world itself that is the incentive, or that in which reason originally would take an interest; but to make this comprehensible is precisely the problem that we cannot solve.

Now here is the supreme boundary of all moral inquiry; to determine it, however, is already of great importance, so that, on the one side, reason, in a way harmful to morality, does not look around in the world of sense for the supreme motivation and for a comprehensible but empirical interest, but on the other side, so that, in what for it is the empty space of transcendent concepts, under the name of the intelligible world, it does not beat its wings powerlessly, without moving from the spot and losing itself among figments of the mind. Besides, the idea of a pure world of the understanding, as a whole of all intelligences, to which we belong as rational beings (although on the other side at the same time members of the world of sense) is always a usable and permissible idea on behalf of a rational faith,[a] even if at its boundary all knowledge has an end, in order to effect a lively interest in the moral law in us through the splendid ideal of a universal realm of *ends in themselves* (rational beings), to which we can belong as members only when we carefully conduct ourselves in accordance with maxims of freedom as though they were laws of nature.

[Ak 4:463]

Concluding remark

The speculative use of reason, *in regard to nature,* leads to the absolute necessity of some supreme cause *of the world;* the practical use of reason, *in regard to freedom,* also leads to absolute necessity, but only *of the laws of actions* of a rational being as such. Now it is an essential *principle* of every use of our reason to drive its cognition to the consciousness of its *necessity* (for without this it would not be cognition of reason). But it is also just as essential a *limitation* of precisely the same reason, that it can gain no insight into either the necessity of what exists or what happens, nor into that which ought to happen, unless grounded on a *condition* under which it exists, or happens, or ought to happen. In this wise, however, the satisfaction of reason is always deferred through the constant questioning after the condition.[9] Hence it seeks restlessly the unconditionally necessary and sees itself necessitated to assume it, without any means of making it comprehensible; it is fortunate enough if it can only discover the concept that is compatible with this presupposition. Thus it is no fault of our deduction of the supreme principle of morality, but only an accusation that one

a. *Glaubens*[8]

would have to make against human reason in general, that it cannot make comprehensible an unconditioned practical law (such as the categorical imperative must be) as regards its absolute necessity; for we cannot hold it against reason that it does not will to do this through a condition, namely by means of any interest that grounds it, because otherwise it would not be a moral, i.e. a supreme, law of freedom. And thus we indeed do not comprehend the practical unconditioned necessity of the moral imperative, but we do comprehend its *incomprehensibility,* which is all that can be fairly required of a philosophy that strives in principles up to the boundary of human reason.

Notes

1. According to Diogenes Laertius, *Lives and Opinions of the Eminent Philosophers* 7.39, this division was first devised by Zeno of Citium (335–265 B.C.) and was characteristic of the Stoics. Cf. Seneca, *Epistles* 89.9; Cicero, *De Finibus* 4.4.
2. Cf. KrV, A50–55/B74–79.
3. Christian Wolff (1679–1754), *Philosophia Practica Universalis* (1738–1739). Kant uses the same title himself, however, as a subtitle to the section of the introduction to the *Metaphysics of Morals* entitled "Preliminary Concepts of the Metaphysics of Morals" in which he discusses concepts such as freedom, duty, personhood, maxims, and laws (MS 6:221–228).
4. Kant's *Metaphysics of Morals*, MS 6:205–493, was published in 1797–1798.
5. Kant published the *Critique of Practical Reason*, KpV 5:1–163, in 1788. But he appears not to have intended to write a separate work with that title in 1785–1786. He apparently planned to include a "practical" section in the second edition of the *Critique of Pure Reason* (1787), but published the *Critique of Practical Reason* separately when it grew too long for that.

1. See *Anthropology from a Pragmatic Point of View*, Anth 7:196–201.
2. For Kant's distinction between 'temperament' and 'character', see Anth 7:286–295; see also G 4:398–399 below.
3. Power, wealth, and honor are for Kant the three objects of the principal social passions. See Anth 7:271–274.
4. The phrase "rational and impartial spectator" is drawn from the moral philosophy of Adam Smith (1723–1790). The sentiments and judgments made from the standpoint of a rational (or fair) impartial spectator are regarded by Smith as the proper standard for the moral judgment of actions,

persons, and characters. See Smith, *The Theory of Moral Sentiments* (1759), III.I.2–6.

5. In Kant's empirical theory of the faculty of desire, affects and passions are the two principal obstacles to rational self-control. See MS 6:407–409; Anth 7:251–267.

6. Courage and self-control for the ancients were two of the primary moral virtues, along with wisdom, justice, and sometimes piety. See Plato, *Meno* 78d–e; *Republic* 427e; Aristotle, *Nicomachean Ethics* 3.6–12; Cicero, *On Duties* 1.15.

7. Kant's reasons for accepting this proposition as an *a priori* maxim of reflective judgment are presented in the *Critique of the Power of Judgment* (1790), § 66, KU 5:376–377.

8. Kant rejects the proposition that human happiness is an end of nature in his writings on history and in his review of the chief work of his former student J. G. Herder (1762–1802). See I 8:19–20; RH 8:64–65; and MA 8:114–118. See also KU 5:429–431. Though not an end of nature, human happiness is an end of reason, and of morality; see KpV 5:61–62, 110–113; MS 6:387–388.

9. See Plato, *Phaedo* 89d–91b.

10. "Luxury (*luxus*) is excessive convenience in the social life of a community (so that its convenience works against its welfare)" (Anth 7:249).

11. Kant does not say explicitly what the "first proposition" was. The usual understanding is that it was: *An action has moral worth only if it is done from duty.* And suppose the third proposition is taken to mean that what we mean when we say an action is done *from duty* is that it is an action performed with necessitation (or self-constraint) through respect for the moral law. (This is explicitly asserted by Kant elsewhere: MS 6:379.) Then the relation between the three propositions might be that

(1) Since an action has moral worth only if done from duty, and

(2) This moral worth consists in the action, not in the value of any end it achieves, therefore

(3) Acting from duty must consist in acting in such a way as to constrain oneself (or from the maxim of constraining oneself) to do the action from respect for law—that is, for the sake of lawfulness in general. This would then facilitate Kant's derivation of the first formula of the moral law from these three propositions, especially from the third, since the formula says that our maxims must be such that they might be willed to be universal laws.

Another suggestion for the first proposition might be this:

(1) *All actions done from duty are actions done from respect for the moral law.* This suggestion has the disadvantage that it has not been stated explicitly, but it has the advantage that what Kant calls the third proposition could be seen to be a logical consequence of it and the second proposition, as Kant may be claiming in the paragraph following this one, at least if we understand the second and third propositions as follows:

(2) an action done from duty follows a maxim required by the moral law.

(3) duties are actions necessitated (or required) by the moral law.

It is less clear on this reading how we get from the third proposition to Kant's first formula, but if the moral law is seen as the principle of all duties, then it might be inferred that the principle of these duties is that law (or lawfulness in general) from respect for which duties might be done.

I think the first of these two readings is the more natural one, but clearly there is more than one possible way to understand Kant's three propositions, the relations between them, and the way they lead to his first formula of the moral law.

12. Cf. KpV 5:71–89. In the *Metaphysics of Morals,* Kant lists *four* feelings that are produced directly by reason and can serve as moral motivation. These are "moral feeling," "conscience," "love of human beings," and "respect" (MS 6:399–403).

13. This would appear to be Kant's interpretation of Socrates' "human wisdom" (Plato, *Apology* 20c–24b). Compare MS 6:411.

SECOND SECTION

1. In *Religion Within the Boundaries of Mere Reason,* Kant lists "fragility" (the inability to hold to good maxims, once they are adopted) and "impurity" (the need for non-moral incentives to do one's duty) as the two lesser degrees of the radical evil in human nature, along with the highest degree: "depravity" (the propensity to place incentives of inclination ahead of those of duty) (R 6:29–30).

2. A likely biblical allusion. Compare: "While we look not at the things which are seen, but at the things which are not seen: for the things that are seen are temporal; but the things which are not seen are eternal" (2 Corinthians 4:18).

3. Once again, a biblical allusion. The phrase *Tichten und Trachten* quotes the Lutheran translation of Genesis 6:5, which reads (in the King James version): "And God saw that the wickedness of man was great in the

earth, and that every imagination of the thoughts of his heart was only evil continually" (cf. also *Genesis* 8:21). This translates the Hebrew *yetzer hara* (יֵצֶר הָרָע) ("inclination to evil"), which was the biblical source of the Augustinian concept of *concupiscentia*. In the *Religion*, Kant equates *concupiscentia* with the radical propensity to evil in human nature (R 6:29). This propensity is not itself a desire (or an "inclination" in Kant's sense of the word), but instead a self-contracted *temptation* toward evil desires (MS 6:213; cf. MS 6:393).

4. See Anth § 2, 7:128–130.

5. "Friendship thought as attainable in its purity or completeness (between Orestes and Pylades, Thesesus, and Pirithous) is the hobby horse of writers of romances. On the other hand, Aristotle says: 'My dear friends, there are no friends!'" (MS 6:470). The statement attributed to Aristotle is based on Diogenes Laertius, *Lives and Opinions of Eminent Philosophers* 5.1.21.

6. The original meaning of 'apodictic' is 'self-evident' (from the Greek 'απο' + 'δεικνυμι'). But Kant more typically uses it in the sense of 'necessary' (this is its apparent meaning in the Table of Judgments, KrV A70/B95); yet an epistemic element of certainty is often intended as well. For example: "Geometrical propositions are all apodictic, i.e. combined with consciousness of their necessity" (KrV B41; cf. A160/B199); "[Mathematical cognition] carries with it thoroughly apodictic certainty (i.e., absolute necessity), hence rests on no grounds of experience" (P § 6, Ak 4:280).

7. "'Why do you call me good?' Jesus answered. 'No one is good except God alone'" (Luke 18:19; cf. Matthew 19:17, Mark 10:18). As in note 2 above, compare also: "While we look not at the things which are seen, but at the things which are not seen: for the things that are seen are temporal; but the things which are not seen are eternal" (2 Corinthians 4:18).

8. Kant's references to "popular philosophy" are primarily allusions to a movement of German Enlightenment philosophers, centered chiefly in Berlin, whose best-known representatives were Christian Garve (1742–1798), Moses Mendelssohn (1729–1786), Christoph Meiners (1747–1810), and Christoph Friedrich Nicolai (1733–1811). Other critical references to this movement can be found throughout Kant's writings (KrV A x, A855/B883; P 4:261–262, 371–383; O 8:133–146; TP 8:278–289; MS 6:206; BM 8:433–437; VL 9:19–20, 148). Despite this, Kant was on terms of friendship and mutual admiration with at least two members of the movement, namely Mendelssohn and Garve. Some scholars have maintained the thesis that Garve's translation, with notes, of Cicero's *De Officiis* greatly influenced the *Groundwork* itself, including its account of the good will and its three formulations of the moral law; see Klaus Reich, "Kant and

Greek Ethics," *Mind* 47 (1939), and A. R. C. Duncan, *Practical Reason and Morality* (London: Nelson, 1957), chapter 11. This thesis, however, is rejected by Reiner Wimmer, *Universalisierung in der Ethik* (Frankfurt: Suhrkamp, 1980), 183–184, and Dieter Schönecker, *Kant: Grundlegung III. Die Deduktion des kategorischen Imperativs* (Freiburg/Munich: Alber Verlag, 1999), 61–67.

9. Johann Georg Sulzer (1720–1779), director of the philosophical division of the Prussian Academy of Sciences (1777–1779). The letter in question is usually thought to be the one dated December 8, 1770 (cf. Ak 13:51), which, however, does not directly raise the question Kant says it does. What Sulzer does say is this:

> I really wished to hear from you whether we may soon hope to see your work on the metaphysics of morals. This work is of the highest importance, given the present unsteady state of moral philosophy. I have tried to do something of this sort myself in attempting to resolve the question, "What actually is the physical or psychological difference between a soul that we call virtuous and one which is vicious?" I have sought to discover the true dispositions of virtue and vice in the first manifestations of representations and sensations, and I now regard my undertaking of this investigation as less futile, since it has led me to concepts that are simple and easy to grasp, and which one can effortlessly apply to the teaching and raising of children. But this work too is impossible for me to complete at present. (Ak 10:112)

10. In his (unpublished) First Introduction to the *Critique of the Power of Judgment* (Ak 20:200 note), Kant retracts the term 'problematical' for this kind of imperative, replacing it with the term 'technical', which he also uses already in the *Groundwork* (G 4:416).

11. Through the use of the word *Ungleichheit,* Kant may be suggesting not only that the three imperatives are different in kind, but also that the three kinds of necessitation have unequal rational weight: moral necessitation is unconditional, hence prior to the other two, overriding them in cases of conflict; pragmatic necessitation by imperatives of prudence, in turn, overrides technical necessitation by imperatives of skill that merely tell us how to achieve some optional end we have contingently chosen.

12. Kant holds that for a well-formed (real) definition of a thing, we require a demonstration of its (real) possibility. See KrV A727–730/B755–759.

13. Cf. MS 6:240, 391–398, 413, and the detailed taxonomy of duties of virtue, MS 6:417–468. The "use of words common in the schools," according to

which perfect duties are externally enforceable actions, is based on Samuel Pufendorf (1632–1694), *De Jure Naturale* (1672), 1.1.19–20. But Pufendorf's distinction was anticipated by Hugo Grotius (1583–1645), and had been taken up also by, among others, Christian Thomasius (1655–1728), J. G. Sulzer, and Moses Mendelssohn.

14. The word *Not* (necessity, distress, emergency) suggests that the agent's maxim is attempting to appeal to the traditional notion of *Notrecht* (right of necessity)—the idea that an action which is usually wrong can be justified or excused under unusual circumstances—of necessity, distress, or emergency. Kant's account of the right of necessity is to be found at MS 6:235–236.

15. In both the 1785 and 1786 editions of the *Groundwork*, and also in the Academy Edition, this word is *Abteilung* ('partitioning' or 'compartmentalizing'). In 1838, Gustav Hartenstein proposed the emendation *Ableitung* ('derivation'). Some other editors, and most English translators, have followed him. Their thought is probably that Kant is repeating the claim he appears to have made at 4:421, that all duties can be derived from the one categorical imperative. But in this paragraph Kant is arguing not for a derivation but a *classification* of duties (according to the maxims that would violate them in these examples): The maxims that violate perfect duties cannot even be thought as universal laws of nature, but the maxims that violate imperfect duties can be thought, but not willed as universal laws of nature. *Abteilung* might be a rather awkward word to use expressing this thought; *Einteilung* ('division, classification') would be a more natural one. But in the very first sentence of the Preface (4:387), Kant himself used the verb *sich abteilen* in a way that, in the second sentence, he seems to equate with *Einteilung*. Further, Kant never in fact attempts to *derive* any duties from either the formula of universal law or the formula of the law of nature. As we will see at G 4:429–430, he does derive these four duties from the formula of humanity as end in itself. So the evidence seems to favor the original wording *Abteilung*.

16. Cf. G 4:439–440 below for the relation between morality and sublimity.

17. Cf. G 4:434 below for the distinction between dignity and price.

18. In Greek mythology, Ixion (a legendary king of Thessaly) schemed to win the love of Hera, queen of the gods (Latin name: Juno). Her husband Zeus discovered his intention and formed a cloud, or cloud nymph, Νεφέλη, that resembled Hera. By the cloud Ixion conceived Centaurus (for which the scholiast gives the false etymology "what penetrates the air"). Centaurus was the ancestor of the centaurs, a race of beings half human and half equine (perhaps Kant's "bastard patched together from limbs of quite diverse an-

cestry" is a reference to them). Zeus punished Ixion for his presumptuous-
ness by having him bound on a wheel in Hades that turns forever. The myth
is told by Pindar, *Pythian Ode* 2.21–50. Since Kant's knowledge of Latin
poetry was better, he is more likely to have known the Ixion story from
Ovid, *Metamorphoses* 4.461, 9.124, 10.42, 12.503–505; Virgil, *Georgics*
3.38, 4.484; or *Aeneid* 6.601, though these later versions emphasize Ixion's
underworld punishment rather than the story of Juno and the cloud.

19. *"Considered in themselves, natural inclinations are good*, i.e. not reprehensible, and to want to extirpate them would not only be futile, but harmful
and blameworthy as well; we must rather only curb them, so that they will
not wear each other out but will instead be harmonized into a whole called
'happiness'" (R 6:58).

20. See MA 8:114; Anth 7:127, 130.

21. This is evidently a reference to 4:448, where Kant argues that every rational will must act under the idea of freedom and thus freedom in a practical
respect must be attributed to all rational beings.

22. *Menschlichkeit;* this term refers to one of our three fundamental predispositions: (1) animality (through which we have instincts for survival,
procreation, and sociability); (2) humanity, through which we have the rational capacities to set ends, use means to them, and organize them into a
whole (happiness); and (3) personality, through which we have the capacity to give ourselves moral laws and are accountable for following them
(see R 6:26–28; Anth 7:322–325). 'Humanity' thus means the same as
'rational nature', and Kant's use of it involves no retraction of the claim
that moral commands must be valid for all rational beings, not only for
members of the human species.

23. In the *Metaphysics of Morals,* Kant discusses the duty not to maim oneself
in connection with the duty forbidding suicide (MS 6:422–423). *Verder-
ben* ('corrupt') therefore probably carries with it the broad sense of ruining
or destroying (sc. one's body or parts of it) rather than the narrower sense
of *moral* corruption. Duties to oneself as a moral being, which Kant classi-
fies as duties against lying, avarice, false humility (or servility), and duties
as moral judge of oneself, are dealt with separately (MS 6:428–442).

24. The application of moral concepts, such as that of this specific duty, to
individual instances, is seen by Kant as the function of the faculty of (determining) judgment, which cannot be reduced to discursive reasoning (see
KrV A132–134/B171–174; TP 8:275; and Anth 7:199.). Kant holds that
judgment is in part an innate talent, but it can be cultivated through experience or the thoughtful consideration of examples, especially those in which
the application of a concept is difficult or problematic. In the *Metaphysics*

of Morals, Kant attempts to encourage the development of this capacity of judgment through "Casuistical Questions," MS 6:411–412; the Casuistical Questions concerning the duty in question here are presented at MS 6:423–424. Notice that the formulas of universal law and law of nature were specifically introduced as a standard or canon of judgment, and at the end of the First Section, Kant considered this specific role of the moral principle to be the only way moral philosophy can serve ordinary moral agents.

25. It is essential to Kant's conception of a promise that it involves a "united will" of the promisor and the promisee (MS 6:272).

26. Here Kant is intentionally distinguishing his principle from the so-called Golden Rule of the Gospels: "Therefore, all things whatsoever ye would that men should do to you, do ye even so to them" (Matthew 7:12; cf. Luke 6:31). Notice that the Latin version Kant quotes is the inverted and negative version: *What you do not want done unto you, do not do unto others.* This has sometimes been called the "Silver Rule." Kant here rejects the identification of this trite moral rule with the fundamental principle of morality, and especially with FH. (By implication, he would seem to reject the identification of FUL with the Golden Rule, though he never says anything explicitly about this either way). Kant, however, does not reject either of these rules themselves; he merely sees them as derivative and conditional applications of the moral principle. In his lectures, Kant even embraces the Silver Rule as among the principles belonging to the laws of a realm of ends (VE Mro 29:611).

27. On the distinction between the "legislator" of a law (who promulgates and attaches sanctions to it), and the "author" of a law (whose will actually imposes the obligation), see MS 6:227. Although Kant frequently speaks here of the rational being as "legislator" of the moral law, his position (more precisely expressed, in this terminology) is that only the rational being who is obligated can be the *author* of the law; Kant allows that we can speak of God (or the "supreme head of the realm of ends") as the *legislator* of the moral law (see below, G 4:433–434; VE Coll 27:282–283; and R 6:99–100).

28. The obvious source for Kant's conception of a "realm of ends" is Leibniz's conception of the "city of God" as the "realm of minds," and the relationship of the "realm of nature" to this "realm of grace." Gottfried Wilhelm Leibniz (1646–1716), *Discourse on Metaphysics* (1686) § 36; *Principles of Nature and Grace Based on Reason* (1714), §15; *Monadology* (1714), §§ 85–90. In his lectures, Kant explicitly identifies the realm of ends with Leibniz's realm of grace (VE Mro 29:611). This formula can also be re-

garded as the first one Kant himself ever used in published writings: "The idea of a moral world . . . a *corpus mysticum* of the rational beings in it, insofar as their free choice under moral laws has thoroughgoing systematic unity in itself as well as with the freedom of everyone else" (*Critique of Pure Reason* A808/B836).

29. See note 27 above.

30. The apparent source for this distinction is Seneca, *Epistles* 71.33. But it is an atypical passage in the Stoic literature, since typically both *pretium* and *dignitas* refer to the value of preferred indifferents rather than to virtue. But compare the following:

> From this we see that sensual pleasure is quite unworthy of the dignity of man [*non satis esse dignam hominis praestantia*]. . . . And if we will only bear in mind the superiority and dignity of our nature [*quae sit in natura excellentia et dignitas*], we shall realize how wrong it is to abandon ourselves to excess and to live in luxury and voluptuousness. . . . We must realize also that we are invested by Nature with two characters [*personis*], as it were: one of these is universal, arising from the fact of our being all alike endowed with reason and with that superiority which lifts us above the brute. From this all morality and propriety are derived, and upon it depends the rational method of ascertaining our duty. (Cicero, *De Officiis* I.xxx.106–107)

31. For the way that the formula of autonomy unites the formula of universal law with the formula of humanity as end in itself, see G 4:431.

32. Concerning the principle of complete determination, see KrV A571–583/B599–611.

33. See KrV A70–71/B95–96, A80/B106.

34. On the sublime, see KU §§ 23–29, 5:248–278; Anth § 68; Ak 7:243.

35. Cf. KrV A xii.

36. Kant associates principles based on physical feeling with the hedonism of Epicurus (341–270 B.C.), principles based on moral feeling with the moral sense theory of Francis Hutcheson (1694–1727), the principle of perfection with Christian Wolff and the Stoics, and principles based on the will of God with the divine command morality of Christian August Crusius (1715–1775) (*Critique of Practical Reason*, Ak 5:40). Kant's fuller taxonomy (KpV 5:40) divides theories of heteronomy into four kinds. "Objective" theories are either (1) "internal" (the theory of perfection) or (2) "external" (divine command theory). (3) "Subjective internal" theories include both the theory of physical and the theory of moral feeling. This

taxonomy makes a place for yet another classification not discussed in the *Groundwork,* namely (4) "subjective external" theories. These include the theory that morality is grounded on education, which Kant associates with Michel Montaigne (1533–1592), and the theory that morality is grounded on the civil constitution, which Kant associates with Bernard Mandeville (1670–1733).

THIRD SECTION

1. See KrV, A7–10/B11–14.
2. Cf. KrV B xv–xxii, A26–30/B42–46, A32–49/B49–73, A490–497/B518–525.
3. Cf. KrV A235–260/B294–315.
4. See KrV A84–130/B116–169.
5. See KrV A293–309/B349–366.
6. Cf. KrV B 162–165.
7. Cf. KrV A532–558/B560–586.
8. See KrV A820–831/B848–859.
9. Cf. KrV A310–340/B366–398, A408–420/B435–448, A497–515/B525–543.

Glossary

Abbruch tun	infringe
ableiten	derive
Absicht	intention; aim
absondern	separate; abstract
Achtung	respect
Affekt	affect
All	(the) all
allgemein	universal; general
Allgemeingültigkeit	universal validity
Allheit	totality
an sich	in itself
anerkennen	recognize
angenehm	agreeable
Anlage	predisposition
Anlockung	enticement
Anmaßung	presumption
Anschauung	intuition
Ansehen	authority
Anspruch	claim
Antrieb	impulse
Arbeit	labor
Art	way, kind, species
auferlegen	impose
Aufgabe	problem
aufheben	abolish
auflösen	resolve, solve; analyze
Aufmunterung	encouragement
aufsuchen	search
ausfindig machen	bring to light
ausmachen	constitute; settle

Bedeutung	significance; signification
Bedingung	condition
Bedürfnis	need
befördern	further; promote
Befugnis	warrant, authorization
begabt	endowed
Begehrungsvermögen	faculty of desire
begreifen	comprehend
Begriff	concept
beharrlich	persisting
beilegen	apply (to), attribute (to)
Belieben	discretion
Bemühung	toil; effort
Berharrlichkeit	persistence
berichtigen	correct
Beschaffenheit	constitution; property
Beschäftigung	enterprise, concern, business
besonder	particular
besorgen	take care
Besorgnis	concern
beständig	permanent, constant
bestimmen	determine
Bestimmung	determination, vocation (in ethical contexts)
betrachten	consider
Betrachtung	inquiry; consideration
Beurteilung	judgment
bewahren	confirm
Bewegungsgrund	motive
Bewegursache	motivation
beweisen	prove
Bewußtsein	consciousness
Beziehung	reference; relation
Bild	image
billig	equitable, fair
billigen	approve
Boden	terrain
Böse	evil
Bösewicht	scoundrel

darlegen	establish
Darstellung	exhibition; presentation; display
dartun	establish
Dauer	duration
Deutlichkeit	distinctness; clarity
Ding	thing
echt	genuine
Ehre	honor
ehrlich	honest; honorable
Eigendünkel	self-conceit
Eigenliebe	self-love
Eigenschaft	quality
eigentlich	real, authentic
einbilden	imagine
Einbildungskraft	imagination
Einfalt	simplicity
Einfluß	influence
einräumen	concede
Einrichtung	adaptation
Einschränkung	limitation
einsehen	have (gain) insight into
einstimmen	harmonize
Empfänglichkeit	receptivity
Empfindung	sensation, feeling
entlehnen	get
Erfahrung	experience
erfordern	require
Erhabenheit	sublimity
Erhaltung	preservation
erheben	elevate
erkennen	cognize, know
Erkenntnis	cognition
Erklärung	explanation; definition; declaration
erlaubt	permissible
Erläuterung	elucidation, illustration
Erscheinung	appearance
erteilen	impart

fähig	susceptible; capable
Fähigkeit	capacity
festsetzen	establish
Freiheit	freedom; liberty
Freundschaft	friendship
Frist	term
Gabe	gift
Gebiet	domain
Gebot	command
Gebrauch	use, employment
Gebrechlichkeit	fragility
gefallen	like, please (v.r.)
gefällig	pleasing
Gefühl	feeling
Gegengewicht	counter-weight
Gegenstand	object
Geist	spirit, mind
Geldnot	financial distress, financial emergency
gemäß	in accord
gemein	common
Gemeinschaft	community (*communio*); interaction (*commercio*)
Gemüt	mind, heart
genugtun	satisfy
Genuss	enjoyment
Geschäft	business, concern, enterprise
gescheit	clever
Geschicklichkeit	skill
Gesetz	law
Gesetzgeber	legislator
Gesetzgebung	legislation; giving law
Gesetzmässigkeit	lawfulness
Gesichtspunkt	point of view
Gesinnung	disposition
Gewalt	control
Gewerbe	trade
Glaube	belief, faith
Glied	member

Glück	(good) fortune; luck
glücklich	happy, fortunate
Glückseligkeit	happiness
Grad	degree
Grenze	bound(ary)
Grund	ground
gründlich	well-grounded
Grundsatz	principle
Gültigkeit	validity
Gunst	favor
Handlung	act(ion)
Hang	propensity
heilig	holy
herrlich	splendid
hervorbringen	produce; bring forth
hinreichend	sufficient
Hirngespinst	figment of the mind
Hochschätzung	esteem
Idee	idea
Imperativ	imperative
Inbegriff	sum total
Kennen	acquaintance
kennen	be acquainted with, know
Kenner	connoisseur
Kenntnis	acquaintance
klar	clear
Klugheit	prudence
Kraft	power; force (physical contexts)
Kritik	critique, criticism
Kunst	art
Laster	vice
Laune	mood
lauten	be stated
lauter	pure
Lehrbegriff	doctrine

Lehre	doctrine
Leidenschaft	passion
liebenswürdig	amiable
Lob	praise
Lüge	lie
Lust	pleasure
Macht	might, power
Materie	matter
meinen	hold or express opinion(s)
Mensch	human being
menschlich	human (adj.)
Menschlichkeit	humanity
Mittel	means
Moral	morals
Moralität	morality
Muster	model
Mut	courage
Nachteil	disadvantage
Naturgesetz	natural law
Neigung	inclination
Not	distress
Nötigung	necessitation
Notwendigkeit	necessity
Nützlichkeit	utility
Oberhaupt	supreme head
oberst	supreme
Object	object
Person	person
Pflicht	duty
pflichtmäßig	in conformity with duty
Preis	price
Prinzip	principle
Prüfung	examination
Quelle	source

Ratgebung	advice
Ratschlag	counsel
Raum	space
Recht	right (n.)
Rechtschaffenheit	uprightness
Redlichkeit	honesty
Regel	rule
Reich	realm
rein	pure
Ruhe	tranquility
Sache	thing
Satz	proposition
Schande	disgrace
schätzen	estimate; esteem
Schätzung	estimation
Schein	illusion; semblance
scheinen	seem
schicklich	suitable
Schlauigkeit	cunning
Schranke	limit(ation)
schwärmen	enthuse
Schwärmerei	enthusiasm
Seele	soul
Selbstbeherrschung	self-control
Selbstbestimmung	self-determination
Selbstliebe	self-love
Selbstmord	suicide
Selbstverleugnung	self-renunciation
Sinn	sense; meaning
Sinnenwelt	world of sense
sinnlich	sensible, sensuous
Sinnlichkeit	sensibility
Sitten	morals, morality
Sittlichkeit	morality
Sollen	'ought'
Standpunkt	standpoint
Stoff	material

Tat	deed
Tätigkeit	activity
Tauglichkeit	suitability
Teilnahme	sympathy; sympathetic participation
Treue	fidelity
Triebfeder	incentive
Tugend	virtue
Tun und Lassen	conduct; deeds and omissions
Übel	ill
Übereinstimmung	agreement
Überlegung	reflection
Übermut	arrogance
übersteigen	surpass
Übertretung	transgression
Überzeugung	conviction
Umfang	range
unbegreiflich	incomprehensible
Unlauterkeit	impurity
unnachlaßlich	unremitting
Unschuld	innocence
unterordnen	subject
Untersuchung	investigation
Unvermögen	incapacity
Urbild	archetype
Urheber	author
Ursache	cause
Urteilskraft	power of judgment
Urwesen	original being
verabscheuen	abhor
verachten	despise
Verachtung	contempt
Veränderung	alteration
Verbindlichkeit	obligation
Verbindung	combination (*conjunctio*)
verdienstlich	meritorious
Vereinigung	unification
Vergnügen	gratification
Verhalten	conduct

Verhältnis	relation
Verkehr	traffic; commercial traffic
Verknüpfung	connection (*nexus*)
Verlegenheit	embarrassment
Vermögen	faculty
vernuenfteln	ratiocinate
Vernunft	reason
verschaffen	obtain
Versprechen	promise
Verstand	understanding
Verstandeswelt	world of the understanding
Versuchung	temptation
verwerflich	reprehensible
Vollendung	completion
vollkommen	perfect (v.)
Vollkommenheit	perfection
vollständig	complete
Vorgeben	pretense
Vorschrift	precept
Vorsorge	provision
vorstellen	represent
Vorstellung	representation (*repraesentatio*)
Vorteil	advantage
wählen	choose
Wahn	delusion
Wahrnehmung	perception
Weg	route
Weltweisheit	philosophy
Wert	worth; value
Wesen	being, entity (*ens*); essence (*essentia*)
Widerspruch	contradiction
Widerstreit	conflict
Wille	will
Willkür	(power of) choice
willkürlich	voluntary; arbitrary
wirklich	actual, real
Wirkung	effect
Wissen	knowledge
Wissenschaft	science

Witz	wit
Wohl	well-being
Wohlergehen	welfare
Wohlgefallen	satisfaction
Wohltun	beneficence
wohltätig	beneficent
Wohlwollen	benevolence
Wollen	volition
wollen	will
Würde	dignity
Zergliederung	analysis
zufällig	contingent
Zufriedenheit	contentment
Zusammenhang	connection; nexus
Zusammensetzung	composition; synthesis
zusammenstimmen	harmonize
Zustand	condition, state
Zwang	coercion
Zweck	end
Zweckmässigkeit	purposiveness

Select Bibliography

Allison, Henry (2011). *Kant's* Groundwork for the Metaphysics of Morals: *A Commentary.* Oxford: Oxford University Press.

Baron, Marcia (1999). *Kantian Ethics (Almost) Without Apology.* Ithaca, NY: Cornell University Press.

Fahmy, Melissa Seymour (2009). "Active Sympathetic Participation: Reconsidering Kant's Duty of Sympathy," *Kantian Review* 14 (1): 31–52.

Guyer, Paul (2014 [2006]). *Kant.* London: Routledge.

Herman, Barbara (1993). *The Practice of Moral Judgment.* Cambridge, MA: Harvard University Press.

Herman, Barbara (2008). *Moral Literacy.* Cambridge, MA: Harvard University Press.

Kant, Immanuel (1999). *Grundlegung zur Metaphysik der Sitten* (1785, 1786). Edited by Bernd Kraft and Dieter Schönecker. Hamburg: Meiner Verlag.

Kant, Immanuel (1902–). *Kants Schriften.* Ausgabe der königlich preussischen Akademie der Wissenschaften. Berlin: Walter de Gruyter. Abbreviated as "Ak" and cited by volume: page.

Korsgaard, Christine (1996a). *Creating the Kingdom of Ends.* Cambridge: Cambridge University Press.

Korsgaard, Christine (1996b). *The Sources of Normativity,* edited by Onora O'Neill. Cambridge: Cambridge University Press.

Korsgaard, Christine (2009). *Self-Constitution.* Oxford: Oxford University Press.

O'Neill, Onora (1989). *Constructions of Reason: Explorations of Kant's Practical Philosophy.* Cambridge: Cambridge University Press.

O'Neill, Onora (2013). *Acting on Principle: An Essay in Kantian Ethics.* Second Edition. Cambridge: Cambridge University Press. First edition: New York: Columbia University Press, 1975.

Rawls, John (2000). *Lectures on the History of Moral Philosophy,* edited by Barbara Herman. Cambridge, MA: Harvard University Press.

Reich, Klaus (1939). "Kant and Greek Ethics I–II," translated by W. H. Walsh. *Mind* 48 (1939): 338–354.

Schönecker, Dieter, and Allen Wood (2015). *Immanuel Kant's* Groundwork for the Metaphysics of Morals: *A Commentary.* Cambridge, MA: Harvard University Press.

Timmermann, Jens (2007). *Kant's* Groundwork of the Metaphysics of Morals: *A Commentary.* Cambridge: Cambridge University Press.

Wood, Allen (1999). *Kant's Ethical Thought.* New York: Cambridge University Press.

Wood, Allen (2008). *Kantian Ethics.* New York: Cambridge University Press.

Wood, Allen (2014). *The Free Development of Each: Studies in Freedom, Right and Ethics in Classical German Philosophy.* Oxford: Oxford University Press.

Wood, Allen (2017). *Formulas of the Moral Law.* Kant Elements. Cambridge: Cambridge University Press.

Index

Note: An *n* following a page number indicates a footnote. An *n* followed by a number indicates an endnote.